Famous Fleets
Volume Six

RAILWAY
ROAD VEHICLES

Alan Earnshaw
&
Bill Aldridge

Trans-Pennine Publishing

CONTENTS

Front Cover: *This Austin K2 has been fully restored and painted in an authentic LMS livery, and is based in Aylesbury.*

Rear Cover Top: *Now part of the National Collection, this Karrier Cob was the doyen of a numerous stud. Registered UR 9869 and bearing fleet number 1-G, the Cob is pictured at the NRM's Railways & Roads Event in 1998.*

Rear Cover Bottom: *Wearing what would have been a crimson lake, white and red livery, this Roe-bodied Leyland Cub entered service with the Huddersfield Joint Omnibus Committee. Charles H. Roe Ltd.*

Title Page: *At the start of the day, a pair of horse-drawn drays leave an ex-L&YR goods yard in 1927 piled high with goods including boxes of Typhoo tea. They are seen passing a line-up of Leyland and Karrier motor lorries waiting to be loaded. LMS Official*

This Page: *This Albion (RO 2050) has a chain-driven rear axle and is fitted with a Derby-built Midland-style cab. The crude cab has canvas side sheets for doors, although other members of this same batch of 'stand dray' lorries did have wooden half-doors. LMS Official*

Opposite Page: *Registered UR 2541, this Karrier has a full width Derby-built cab, as opposed to the three-quarter width version more commonly seen on this chassis. LMS Official*

The **Nostalgia Road** Series ™
is conceived, designed and published
by
Trans-Pennine Publishing Ltd.
PO Box 10
Appleby-in-Westmorland
Cumbria, CA16 6FA
Tel. 017683 51053
Fax. 017683 53558
ISDN. 017683 53684
e-mail trans.pennine@virgin.net
(A Quality Guild registered company)

Reprographics
Barnabus Design & Repro
Threemilestone, Truro
Cornwall, TR4 9AN
01872 241185

And Printed in Cumbria by
Kent Valley Colour Printers Ltd.
Shap Road Industrial Estate
Kendal, Cumbria LA9 6NZ
01539 741344

© Trans-Pennine Publishing & Authors 2001
Photographs: Authors' collections or as credited

INTRODUCTION

This book forms the third part of a series of books detailing the road vehicle operations of the British railway companies. The first book covered *British Railways 1948 - 1968*, whilst the second looked at **GWR Road Vehicles**. In the not too distant future, we will also consider the road vehicle activities of the LNER and the Southern railways. The danger in this (apart from a variety of vehicle types), is repetitiveness as the operation was not hugely dissimilar from one railway to the next. Yet, apart from bus operations (where the GWR took the undoubted lead), the London Midland & Scottish Railway were often the innovators. There are strong indications that the LMS carried out pilot schemes on behalf of, or in association with the other members of the Big Four, and it certainly had the strongest voice when it came to lobbying Parliament on railway road operations.

The pioneer of railway road transport was undoubtedly the Midland Railway, and their vehicles accounted for almost half of the stock taken over by the LMS in the Grouping of 1923. Yet there were other major players, including the Caledonian Railway, The Glasgow & South Western, and the combined fleet of the London & North Western and Lancashire & Yorkshire railways that had 'merged' on 1st January 1922 as a prelude to the Grouping a year later.

My own interest in the subject comes from a family involvement in railway cartage, and also a fascination in an integrated transport system. As a keen railway modeller, I also like to see accurate road models incorporated in the scenes portrayed, as the out of scale but ubiquitous 'Matchbox' model looked completely incongruous on what were otherwise excellently produced scale models. The advent of more realistic scale road vehicles, such as EFE and Corgi (for 4mm), has done much to improve this situation, but the railway modeller still needs that degree of inspiration in order to have precisely the right type of vehicle on their display.

Yet the book does not ignore social history, and I hope that the experiences of some of those LMS drivers and car-men that we have included in one chapter of this book, will present a fascinating view of life on the railways in days when they offered an all-encompassing service to the public. Meanwhile, bus enthusiasts will not be disappointed, and (whilst we are looking at further volumes on railway buses), this publication does not ignore the subject. I trust that it will therefore provide a work of reference to the reader, and a source of inspiration to the modeller, but above will be a fascinating trip down Nostalgia Road for all those who progress beyond the cover pages.

Alan Earnshaw   Appleby-in-Westmorland, March 2001

The LMS Constituents

This book begins life on 1st January 1923, and ends on 31st December 1947, and covers one of the largest joint-stock railway companies ever known. The formation of the London Midland & Scottish Railway was, along with the other Big Four companies, a political act and a direct response to the events of World War I. This situation had come about because the railways had been taken under the Government control through the Railway Executive Committee on 5th August 1914. In the dark years that followed, the railways were literally the life-blood of the nation, and they helped sustain both military and civilian needs.

The role that the railways played during this period of time is completely understated, and I have to assert that without their efforts, the course of the Great War would have been completely different from its eventual outcome. To understand this statement, readers would need to see my book *Britain's Railways At War*, published by Atlantic Transport Publishers.

Not only did they supply large amounts of equipment and munitions through their workshops, but they also supplied much equipment for military use. This included cross-channel ferries, locomotives, rolling stock, and horse-drawn vehicles. Even entire branch lines were ripped up, shipped to France and re-laid to provide communication routes behind the front lines.

Above: *Numbered 46 in the Lancashire & Yorkshire Railway road vehicle fleet, this 30cwt Albion was allocated to the Carriage & Wagon works at Newton Heath, Manchester.* LMS Official

Back at home the railways carried inordinate amounts of military equipment and an ever-increasing level of civilian traffic. Yet, despite swingeing cuts in services (over 400 station closures and stringent civilian travel restrictions), the railways were unable to cope with the workload placed upon both them and their road delivery fleet. Yet, with typical British aplomb, the railways muddled through and presented a near normal service. Staff and material shortages were ever present, and by September 1916 no less than 476 locomotives were stopped nationally awaiting major overhaul. Yet despite this, by the spring of 1918 civilian traffic was up 22% on the corresponding period in 1913, and the number of 'express parcels' being moved by the road delivery fleets was up a staggering 63%. This was in addition to all the military traffic being conveyed on the Government's account.

This led to a rapid 'wearing down' of the system, yet the levels of compensation 'agreed' before the State Control of railways was achieved did not cover the costs of reinstatement. Therefore the position after the Armistice was quite unfavourable to the railways of Britain, and it was obvious that massive state intervention would be required even to maintain the status-quo.

As it was, the Government stopped short of absolute state control by means of nationalisation, and it therefore opted to promote a grouping of the railways into four major companies. In all 130 separate railways would be 'grouped' into the 'Big Four' companies, namely the LMS, GWR, LNER and Southern. In the case of the LMS, the railways absorbed were:-

Arbroath & Forfar Rly.
Caledonian Rly.
Cathcart District Rly.
Cleator & Workington Junc Rly.
Dearne Valley Rly.
Dundee & Newtyle Rly.
Glasgow & South Western Rly.
Highland Rly.
Knott End Rly.
Lancashire & Yorkshire Rly.
London & North Western Rly.
Midland Rly.
North & South Western Jun Rly
North Staffordshire Rly.
Shropshire Union Rly.
Stratford upon Avon & Midland Junction Rly.
Tottenham & Forest Gate Rly.
Wirral Rly.

Brechin & Edzell District Rly.
Callander & Oban Rly.
Charnwood Forest Rly.
Cockermouth, Keswick & Penrith
Dornock Light Rly.
Furness Rly.
Harborne Rly.
Killin Rly.
Lanarkshire & Ayrshire Rly.
Leek & Manifold Light Rly.
Maryport & Carlisle Rly.
Mold & Denbigh Junction Rly.
North London Rly.
Portpatrick & Wigtownshire Joint
Solway Junction Rly.
Wick & Lybster Light Rly.
Yorkshire Dales Rly.

Many of these railways had developed road vehicle services, although a few had just experimented with the operation. The smaller ones had originated 'cartage' contracts with outside contractors supplying the road vehicles, but others had been very progressive in the development of their road fleet. In this respect the LNWR, L&YR and Midland can be looked to as shining examples. The L&YR in particular were very proactive in the development of road motor vehicles, but this is hardly surprising when one considers the hilly terrain in which their horse-drawn vehicles had to operate. The fact that road motor vehicle manufacturers like Ford and Leyland were based within their territory undoubtedly helped, but to start we must consider the horse operation.

Top Right: *The real development in parcel traffic delivery and collection came with the Midland Railway's horse-drawn parcels service. This standard Midland collecting van, No. 565, is typical of the type of van used throughout the system and was later developed as the LMS Type 1 van.* S. Shelton Collection

Middle Right: *A development of the horse-van came with electric traction, as exampled by this Ransome, Sims & Jeffries parcels van which Derby purchased from Mossay Electric Vehicles. This mock-up picture was created to show advertising panels.* S. Shelton Collection

Bottom Right: *Again fitted with a Derby body, we see the next stage in the story, in the shape of a 1³/4-ton Morris Commercial motor lorry for the Midland & Great Northern Joint Rly.* S. Shelton collection

The Horse Operation

To describe the LMS railway horse operation would take a book in its own right, and some may argue that the subject has no place within a book aimed at road vehicle enthusiasts. Yet whilst this series is predominantly concerned with the development of the road motor vehicle and its use, neither can we forget the forebearers upon which many famous fleets were developed. Nowhere is this more true than in the railway road vehicle fleet, where the horse maintained a major position for over 100 years and lasted in regular daily use (in appreciable numbers) down into the 1950s. In fact the horse gave rise to many terms still in use on the railways today, and as an example we might turn to the fact that locomotive drivers still 'stable' their engines or multiple units at the end of their working day. The horse was there at the dawn of railways, and a glance at the reverse side of a British five pound note confirms this, as a horse and flagman are depicted preceding *Locomotion* across the Skerne Bridge at Darlington in September 1825.

Above: *Fleet number 26H was a $2^{1}/4$-ton open van that was used for carrying animal feed. It was allocated to the Camden Goods Depot in London, and is seen here in August 1927 after winning first place in a company competition.* S. Shelton Collection

However, as the iron horse spread out across the realm from those first beginnings of a public railway service at Darlington, its use as a means of mass-transit soon led to the gradual demise of horse-drawn services. Yet the horse still had a vital role to play, and in the days of the embryonic railways, it provided a vital link to the communities surrounding the railways. Furthermore, it would continue to do so until the railways found a means of penetrating the hinterland and offering a direct service to the populace. In fact horse-drawn road services remained an important part of Britain's transport infrastructure for up to 50 years after the opening of the Stockton & Darlington in 1825. In rural areas, especially where the railways decided not to construct lines, the use of horse-drawn transport continued until well after the end of World War II.

Top Right: *Looking at modern-tipper lorries of today, we might not instantly recognise this horse-drawn cart as once being a common example of a vehicle performing a similar function. However the LMS had a large number of 13-cwt tipper carts, and a smaller number of 15-cwt tippers. The 15-cwt version, number 22587, achieved extra capacity by having 'side board' extensions.* LMS Official

Middle Right: *Here we see another 2¹/₄-ton open van, No. 297, employed in town cartage. It is carrying amongst other items, boxes of 'Lifebuoy' carbolic soap, just the stuff to have a good rub down in the tin bath before the scullery fire after a long hard day at the mill. Note also the advert for the neat, pilfer-proof Gumstop parcel tape. How times have changed!* S. Shelton Collection

Bottom Right: *Although built at Wolverton (the ex-LNWR carriage works), this 2¹/₄-ton open van was constructed to a Midland design. Note it has a high driver's seat (designed for city centre work) along with much smaller wheels than the previously illustrated 2¹/₄-ton open vans, it is also fitted for twin-horse working. Quite why No.22580 was fitted out like this is not known, but Arfon Roberts thinks they may have been an experimental arrangement.* LMS Official

The railway horse therefore formed the bridge between the fixed railway infrastructure and the communities/industries that surrounded it. It was a vital bridge because, as many readers will appreciate, the railways and their stations were often built several miles from the communities they purported to serve. This was done for reasons of geography, and achieved at a time when the pace of life was much slower than today. Furthermore in the early days of the industrial revolution people were far more ready to walk than they are now. However as the movement of people and goods became more commonplace, the emphasis on delivery times, waiting times and distances to the nearest station became increasingly more important.

As it was financially impractical (and often physically impossible) to provide railways in every community, the operating companies began to look at ways of providing connecting services. In our companion book, *GWR Railway Road Vehicles*, we have discussed how this dilemma was faced by the Great Western Railway at a time when every community demanded its own connection to the national railway network. The adoption of inter-connecting bus services rapidly grew, as the level of investment in a road motor bus fleet was substantially lower than would have been required to build new branch lines. The same policy had been implemented many years earlier by railways who would later become the major constituents in the LMS, but in their case this investment was with respect to providing connecting freight services.

Oddly enough, whilst similar types of service evolved, the underlying reasons for providing the service differed considerably. For example the Midland Railway, fighting to establish itself in areas often packed with competing railway companies, expanded its horse-drawn delivery and collection fleet considerably. In the 30 years from 1860 to 1890, the horse stud grew from just a few animals to over 3,000.

Top Left: *This was a non-standard LMS type 24 dray, based on a Midland Railway design and used only in London. Number 22480 was a two-horse dray that had a carrying capacity of 5-tons. It was fitted with a high driving position and also side raves which were useful in retaining loads like barrels or kegs. It spent most of its working life at Willsden, but it is also known to have been at St. Pancras and Camden at various times.* LMS Official

Middle Left: *This was a low-loading, small-wheeled wagon with a capacity of 3-tons. Although seen here with a large packing case, wagons like No.6512 generally hauled container traffic. Note the three horse team.* R. Fysh Collection

Bottom Left: *Once again, with a high driving seat, we see another 'town dray'. This one, No.22653, has a carrying capacity of 6¼-ton and as a result is fitted with short-spoked wheels. Note the very solid nature of the headboard.* LMS Official

In more rural areas, such as the South West of Scotland (served by the Glasgow & South Western Railway), or the Pennines (served by the Lancashire & Yorkshire Railway), the story was somewhat different. In this type of district, where the territory was often sparsely populated and predominantly rural, a single railway would often have a monopoly. The emphasis was therefore not on competition, but consolidation. As a result the company would seek to expand its services into the outlying districts in order to prevent incursions by possible competitors. These services were usually horse-operated, although branch lines, light railways and even tramways were constructed where the traffic justified the expenditure.

Using the railway as a central corridor from which passengers, goods and the mail could be transmitted into a wider area, the collection and delivery service was often provided by astute farmers or carriers who saw the arrival of the railway as a new market. Many of the local farmers, who supplied horses and carts to the contractors building the railways, became cartage agents to the railways once the lines were opened. Such was the case with my own great, great grandfather who supplied four horse-drawn wagons during the building of the London & North Western Railway tunnel at Standedge, and later went on to become a railway cartage agent with 22 wagons, two horse-drawn omnibuses, and also the local horse-drawn ambulance.

Cartage agents were around from the birth of the railways, and in the early days of the London & Birmingham Railway, no less than 15 agents operated services from 17 different points on that line, each of which serviced the hinterland of the L&B rail corridor. These firms would collect or deliver goods in a wide area, and use the railway as the link to and from the major centres of population. In this instance the L&B would charge the contractor a rate for the rail portion of the journey, but left it to the individual operator to fix their own scale of charges for the job. This policy began to change following two pieces of legislation, namely the Railway Clauses Act of 1845 and the Railway & Canal Act of 1854.

These two Acts regularised various anomalies in the railways nationally, and thereafter the railways were obligated to act as common carriers. This meant that there was a requirement for the railways to afford reasonable facilities for the receiving, forwarding and delivery of goods, no matter what its type and nature. It also brought about freedom of access to outside contractors, who thereafter could deliver or collect from stations and goods yards without severe restrictions being imposed by the operating company. To ensure an overall co-ordination of services meeting a set of operating criteria, the railways then took over many of the former cartage agent operations, especially those in the larger towns and cities. In other areas they appointed official cartage agents, using them as sub-contractors to the railways, often painting their vehicles in railway colours or displaying the railway name.

In many areas it was not profitable for the railway to offer an exclusive company-owned service, and the cartage agents therefore had freedom in offering other services as well; as can be seen by my family operation, which included omnibuses and ambulances. Nevertheless, it was from this period onwards that the railway-owned horse service flourished. The companies analysed the types of traffic they carried and the districts they served, and structured planning was introduced both in terms of operation and the acquisition of new vehicles. The desire to have more and more new vehicles to cope with the growing levels of traffic also gave opportunity to standardise on the types of vehicle within the railway fleet. As a result standard types and standard components came to be employed, thus making both maintenance and operation considerably easier.

Some of the new vehicles were obtained from outside coachbuilders, but rapidly the railways began to realise that they could satisfy their own needs by using their own workshop facilities. A few enterprising railways like the LNWR and the L&YR even built horse-drawn vehicles for other railway companies. In fact, as part of the National Defence Act of 1888, the Midland and GWR horse drawn wagon designs were identified for use as military transportation. A further consideration was made that, by part funding the construction of wagons for railway use, they would be available to the army in times of national emergency.

Top Right: *This view shows a 4-ton ST30 trolley built to a Midland Railway design, fitted with steel-rimmed wooden wheels on the front axle and solid rubber wheels on the rear axle. This illustration shows the turntable arrangement which carried the front axle. In later years, it would be the adaptation of the front turntable that would allow such vehicles to be used with Mechanical Horses.* LMS Official

Middle Right: *Here we see a 4-ton pair-horse dray about to receive a C-type container. Meanwhile the two horses take the opportunity to enjoy a respite as they eat from their feed bags.* S. Shelton Collection

Bottom Right: *This is a Midland standard model, which was refurbished in September 1931, when it was fitted with rubber tyres on the rear axle.* LMS Official

Top Left: *A fascinating example of goods handling is seen in this*

view of bales of cotton being wound off a stand trailer (No.5792) on to what seems to be a chain-driven Albion lorry. R. Fysh Collection

Middle Left: *A couple of pair-horse 4-ton open vans Nos. 6347 and 6372, both with tilts (canvas covers) carrying advertising for LMS services.* R. Fysh Collection

Bottom Left: *At the start of the day, a trio of open vans (Nos.1301, 1309 and 1205) leave Camden Depot for work in Central London.* R. Fysh Collection

Top Right: *A trio of Morris Commercial lorries (JH 2118, JH 2131 and 2132) seen collecting textile machinery which is being exported from a factory in Lancashire in the late 1920s. It is interesting to note that the loads on two of the twin rear-axled lorries are not in packing crates.* LMS Official

The railway horse reigned supreme until well into the 20th Century, despite the advent of both electric traction and the internal combustion engine. Furthermore, the range of special horse-drawn equipment grew substantially, as did facilities for the care and management of the horse stud. Stables where provided wherever horses were required, and even very small stations or goods yards had their own facilities. Larger stables had their own smithy and many had a 'first aid' station. More serious cases would be dealt with at a horse hospital, and the LMS owned such facilities at Kentish Town, Willesden, Manchester, Birmingham, Derby, Leeds and Glasgow. Detailed instructions for the care of horses were provided in a booklet entitled *Instructions To Carters, Attendants and Stable Staff.* The LMS also made their own feed stuff, owning provendor mills at Camden (London), Oakham (Rutland), Manchester and Glasgow.

By the eve of World War I, the horse vehicle fleet of the LMS constituents stood at almost 20,000 (19,773), almost 50% of which had been purchased by the Midland. The growth of the road motor fleet had already made some inroads into the horse stud, as improvements in the reliability and durability of internal combustion engined vehicles had shown that an alternative to the horse was available. The further improvements that came about in commercial vehicles as a result of World War I were also significant, but despite what some commentators have said, this was not the real reason why the railways began to replace horses with commercial motor vehicles.

At the outset of the war, thousands of railway horses and wagons were requisitioned for military use (army and navy), and 12% of the (national) railway horse stud was taken over by the Government in the first year of the war. By the end of 1916, almost 45% had been taken, along with 37% of the horse-drawn wagon fleet. Major dispatches of such material went from stations like Ormskirk on the L&YR. As very little of this material was returned at the end of the conflict, it presented the railway companies with a unique opportunity to completely modernise rather than replace like for like.

The horse-drawn vehicle fleet operated by the LMS can be roughly

divided into a series of vehicle types; as these had a bearing on the motor vehicle types that followed, we will give a brief over-view of the various models employed.

First of all there were the drays and flat trolleys, in which there were two sub-types. Then came the steel-tyred vehicle, which had a capacity ranging from 1³/4-tons to 10-tons; then came the trolleys and drays with pneumatic tyres in the 2¹/4-tons to 3¹/4-tons range. These drays were often built with bodies specific for the type of traffic to be carried, or for the towns in which they would be operated. For example, in those towns with dense traffic, the car-man's seat would be positioned higher than normal; meanwhile, for other types of traffic, e.g. textiles, higher head or tail boards would be used. The drays or trolleys would also be built in different haulage configurations, so that either one or a multiple number of horses could be used. Not all of these vehicles were made of wood, and welded steel began to make an appearance before World War I. The next group to consider were the floats, carts and open vans that were used in large numbers. The open van had been very well used by the LNWR and Midland railways, and these vehicles gave the driver excellent visibility and could achieve a considerable degree of speed around the city.

The open cart tended to have a lot of internal-use work, and

several were built as tip carts. There was a large variety of other vehicles for 'internal-use', but as these were not generally termed as 'revenue-earning', they have not been included in this book. Floats were generally to a 3-ton or 4-ton capacity and were ideally suited for carrying items that could not be moved by the dray. Fitted with extending boards, the floats were often used to carry livestock, including some on a 'by road throughout' basis.

Covered parcels vans were generally associated with the fast traffic carried by passenger trains, therefore most of these vans were painted in the Express Parcels Traffic livery. The ultimate development of the parcel van was a light-weight body on a strong (but light-weight frame), and employed pneumatic tyres. As Ron Buckland recalls, 'these vans could really move, and in the hands of a good driver they could also show motor vehicles a thing or two.' These same vans would be used for cartage work, as well as offering a 'cash on delivery' service to mail order supply companies. On these jobs the driver could collect up to £100 per consignment (about £6,000 at today's prices) on behalf of the sender. The final group of vehicles were the timber carriages, which as their name implies were used to convey supplies of timber, but were used for a whole variety of jobs, including the movement of circus tentage and naval guns!

The Developing Road Motor Fleet

As stated in the preceding chapter, the development of the road motor vehicle within the railway operation was not rapidly achieved. The very size and complexity of the railway horse stud saw to that, and it had to be a very brave manager who would suggest any challenge to the supremacy of the railway horse. The sheer level of investment that had been placed in the horse service, almost single-handedly, ensured that the motor vehicle presented no serious challenge to the horse operation.

Therefore it was only for special operations that motor vehicles were initially bought, although there is evidence that several motor cars were purchased and allocated to senior members of staff for personal use. The motor car soon ousted the pony and trap from these duties, and there seemed to be a great deal of prestige associated in calling upon a customer in their very own automobile. Consequently, the use of cars soon spread to senior goods and passenger agents, inspectors, and others who had to travel on railway company commercial activity. On the cartage side of the railway operation, the LNWR, L&YR and MR all began to experiment with road haulage.

Above: *These Northrop looms are bound from Blackburn to Barcelona, and the first stage of the journey is by LMS lorry. From left to right Karrier JH 3206, AEC JH 3642 and Karrier JH 3202.* LMS Official

Indeed, considerable fleets were built up by these companies, but when one looks at the fleet lists three things are immediately obvious.
1. The fleets included a wide variety of vehicle types, but had few numbers within a given type, thus creating conclusive evidence that purchases of motor lorries and vans was by means of experiment and not a major change in policy.
2. In relation to the numbers of horse-drawn vehicles, the road motor fleets (despite being sizeable) were in fact quite minuscule when the operation was taken as a whole.
3. In considering factors one and two, and despite the fact that horse-haulage was obviously cheaper at the time, the railways had done a SWOT Analysis (strengths, weaknesses, opportunities, threats) of road haulage and decided to gain their own operating experience in this alternate form of transportation.

Top Right: *The Lancashire & Yorkshire Railway were very much at the forefront of motor vehicle development, and at an early stage two companies within their territory approached them to experiment with motor vehicles. These firms were Leyland Motors and the Ford Motor Company (then based at Trafford Park in Manchester); this is one of the Ford Model-T vans used on Express Parcel Traffic.* LMS Official

Middle Right:*Looking superb at Newton Heath workshops, this brand new 4-ton Leyland lorry has solid tyres on spoked wheels at the rear and pressed-disc wheels at the front. Number 49 in the L&YR fleet it has a Manchester registration number NA 8048 which was allocated in 1913.* LMS Official

Bottom Right: *Here we see another model used by the L&YR, this time a Lacre chassis carrying an express parcels body in 1912. Note the advertisement for the L&YR's North Sea ferry service from Hull to Rotterdam and Zebrugge.* LMS Official

As stated earlier, the biggest factor that influenced change was the advent of World War I, which in turn impacted on the railways in the following ways.

1. It brought greater than ever volumes of traffic, much of which required cartage or delivery by the Express Parcels service.
2. It reduced the number of men working in the cartage/delivery service, and therefore resulted in a need for mechanisation.
3. It brought large numbers of female workers into the service, which also resulted in a need for mechanisation.
4. It brought about a number of station closures, which resulted in extending delivery areas from the remaining stations.
5. The Government, who controlled all transport facilities, demanded greater use of mechanised transport, especially on those routes linking the new war factories with the railhead.
6. The large volume of railway horses and carts requisitioned by the military gave the railways real problems in maintaining the cartage operation. Motor vehicles were therefore made available for 'home use', as the horse proved to be eminently more useful in the foreign theatres of war, especially in the mud-swamped battlefields of Western Europe. Motor vehicle manufacturers were therefore directed to supply lorries and vans to essential users like the railway companies, as 'a matter of national importance.'

The period following 'the war to end all wars' left the railways in ruin, the massive backlog of maintenance and inadequate compensation all coupled with the horrendous inflation that followed. The 8-hour day also had a massive impact at a time when a new challenge, road haulage, was beginning to present a threat to what had hitherto been an almost exclusive monopoly on the part of the railways. The companies obviously recognised the threat, but there was little they could do about it. Hundreds of motor lorries that had been built for the army, or imported from the USA, were sold at 'knock-down prices' once the conflict ended. Men who had been trained as drivers in the armed forces seized the opportunity and hundreds of new haulage firms were started.

Top Left: *Typical of the type of lorry used by the railway companies after World War I, this AEC Y-Type (LU 9608) was purchased from the War Department by the LNWR. It is seen here as No.117B in the LMS fleet in 1924 as it is being loaded with a B-type container.* S. Shelton Collection

Middle Left: *Over the years the railway companies persisted with the use of electric road traction, and they considerably helped in the development of road vehicles by working alongside various manufacturers. This vehicle was supplied to the Midland Railway by Mossay Electrical Vehicles, but it seems to carry a number of American-designed features.* S. Shelton Collection

Bottom Left: *Registered CH 1239, Midland Railway No.7375 was a Star 1^1/2-ton petrol lorry.* S. Shelton Collection

The railways reacted to the opposition, but often too slowly to prevent the competition from becoming properly established. However, it was not all 'a bed of roses' for the one-man haulier in those days, and many of the new businesses failed or resorted to 'dubious means' in order to survive. One such story is told in the Neville Shute novel, *Lonely Road,* and is based upon a true story of a driver who became involved with a gun-running gang in order to make ends meet.

In other cases the railways did manage to sort out their services, often quite dramatically. One of the best examples of consolidation that I have come across was told to me by A. J. Ludlam from South Africa. At the end of World War I he was working as a goods clerk at Holmfirth Station in the West Riding of Yorkshire, where the company used the services of an outside cartage agent. For years, probably since the opening of the station in 1850, the delivery of goods or passengers' parcels was done by a local firm of haulage contractors. These agents used horse-drawn vehicles and rented stables from the L&YR, which were located on the lane leading down from the station yard. He recalls:-'In 1918 the agents were the Middleton Brothers, who exclusively handled all the L&YR traffic over a large area and were paid at a fixed rate. This was worked out by the company who gave free delivery to customers for anything within a radius of one mile, an extra amount was charged for deliveries up to two miles, whilst anything beyond that distance had an even higher charge. Though the first mile was covered by the L&YR, any charges for additional mileage were a matter between the contractor and the recipient. Up to 1916 the charges and rates had roughly remained the same, as had wages and rents, but during the war (when price increases became a frequent occurrence) the contractor had asked for, and received, regular increases in his tariff.

By 1919 it had become his habit to ask for more at the end of each December and June, notifying the L&YR he needed the increase or he would have to stop collecting and delivering. Usually the price-increase was accepted without question, despite the fact that the increase was not always justified. Midway through 1920 he gave one month's notice of another hike in his prices, but this time he did not get a reply from Manchester as he had always done.

On the last day of July a worried Joe Middleton came up to see Station-master Moxon, and the three of us were stood on the platform outside the office discussing the possible reasons why the L&YR had not replied to his notice. From where we were stood you could see the road from Huddersfield quite clearly, and as we talked a procession of five or six goods vehicles were coming along the road towards Holmfirth. Not many minutes later all the vehicles pulled up in the station yard opposite. All were brand new, and all were boldly lettered L&YR and Mr Moxon said "Well Joe - there's your answer!" When the convoy arrived, the man in charge asked Mr. Moxon to inform the contractor to vacate his premises immediately so that they could be used for garaging the new motor vehicles, and also tell him that, from thereon the company would be doing it's own carting.' Mr Ludlam would not give a detailed description of the contractor's reaction, but he said 'Never before or since have I ever heard anything to compare with his outburst!'

All the lorries, except a Leyland 1-ton parcel van, were brand new Peerless 4-toners, which had been bought as surplus from the American Army stores near Liverpool. As there had been very few motor lorries in the area before and never any on the railway, Mr. Ludlam said; 'It was fortunate that the labour exchange were able to help us. There had been quite a few local men who had learned to drive in the Army, and having recently been demobilised they had just signed-on. The quick development of the railway's road transport service really took off after 1921 and was helped along by these war surplus vehicles which were assigned to work from all the outlying stations in the L&YR's Huddersfield district.'

This was typical of the situation at many stations in the aftermath of World War I, and by the time of the Grouping the railways had begun to consolidate its road haulage operation. The logic is understandable, and it made far greater sense to absorb a contractor rather than let him expand on the back of high profits from railway traffic, and then launch out to offer a competing service. However, several agents did just that, and many well-known haulage companies began life this way.

Top Right: *As mentioned in the text, Holmfirth was the base for five Peerless lorries. Here one of the ex-USA Army lorries trundles past Kaye's Ironmongers. Years later, the BBC would film this part of the town as the location of Sid's Cafe in the* Last of The Summer Wine *television series.* Huddersfield Examiner

Middle Right: *Another model bought by the L&YR in large numbers was the Albion chain-driven chassis. This view once again shows RO 2050 in LMS livery, but this time a year after the view on page 2 and after crude side doors had been fitted to the cab.* LMS Official

Bottom Right: *A slightly more modern batch of Albion chassis were purchased by the LMS between 1928 and 1932, as exampled by UR 4948. Acquired as fleet number 1818B in 1929, this 5-ton Albion M35 (chassis no.8011F) was fitted out as a two-deck sheep transporter and entered service in February 1930.* S. Shelton Collection

Top Left: *In considering the experimental types of road vehicles used by the LMS constituent companies, the trio of pictures on this page helps to illustrate the type of development undertaken. Firstly we see another Midland Railway electric dray, again supplied by Mossay. Fleet number 192 (CH 1274) was a 2-ton electric dray based on a Ransome, Sims and Jeffries design and capable of speeds up to 12mph.* S. Shelton Collection

Middle Left: *This Midland Railway steam lorry was of Leyland origin, and rated to a maximum speed of 5mph. It is pictured with a group of women carriage cleaners during World War I.* S. Shelton Collection

Bottom Left: *Painted in LMS livery, and pictured around 1924-5, this Sentinel Standard steam lorry was given fleet number 42A. It is seen here in LMS days whilst carrying parts of a Newcommen beam engine and housing being exported to America after being dismantled.* D.C. Gill Collection

As to the type of vehicle employed, it might have seemed natural for the railways to use steam-powered lorries. Indeed the LNWR, L&YR and MR all experimented with differing types of steam wagon. The LNWR opted for Foden, the Midland chose Leyland, and the L&YR purchased Sentinels. However, of these none were outstanding, and all the Fodens and Leylands had gone by the time of the Grouping. That the L&YR had chosen a little more wisely is recognised by the fact that these survived into LMS ownership, whereas the others had all gone by January 1923.

Electric traction was also very much in favour and the railways, then successfully experimenting with electric rail traction, saw this as an ideal means of developing road services. In 1912 the Midland Railway decided to make an extensive study of the electric vehicles used by Sheffield City Council in its municipal refuse collection services. Where electric vehicles were in use, usually in city centres, they competed effectively with horse-services, and vehicles ranged from 1-ton to 10-tons in capacity. Yet, as the war loomed, the internal-combustion vehicle was aided by yet another unexpected boost. In readiness for the inevitable hostilities, the Government offered subsidies to operators to purchase what it called 'War Department-Approved Chassis'. These vehicles were purchased with the aid of a substantial grant, and also given various subsidies in order to keep them in top-flight condition. Then, if mobilisation was necessary, the owner would sell back the vehicle to the state at a pre-determined price. Few private operators opted for the scheme, but the railways collectively purchased large numbers.

By the end of World War I, the surfeit of surplus motor-lorries put paid to all other forms of traction, and this position carried forward into the formation of the LMS. There was of course a continuing degree of experimentation with electric commercial vehicles that carried on right down into the days of the nationalised railways, but despite the environmental potential that this form of traction still offers, the electric truck never really made its mark.

The type of vehicles purchased at the end of the war reflected the military purchasing position, and makes like AEC and Dennis were quite widespread, but as we have already shown makes like the American Peerless were also common. Yet, with regard to the purchasing policy of the railways, it seems that there was still no preference of one make over another, and this perhaps suggests that acquisitions were still on an 'experiment and evaluate' basis.

The L&YR tended to show a preference to Leyland, but that is hardly surprising given that the Leyland factory was firmly located in L&YR territory. The LNWR and the MR both had an affinity with Claytons, the makers of Karrier Motors. This firm was located in Huddersfield, a town served by three of the main LMS constituents (the LNWR, L&YR and MR). One wonders if there was any connection in this and the fact that the LMS later placed large orders with the firm? The Ford Motor Company, then based in another city served by these three companies (Manchester), was another supplier of railway vehicles. For light duties their Model T was perhaps the only practical option, both on grounds of availability and economy. Other makes like Lacre, Albion, Halley and Willys can all be seen in the fleet lists of the constituent companies. Electric vehicles included famous names like Ransomes Simms & Jeffries, Edison, Electricar, GV and Garrett.

Bodies were occasionally supplied by outside coachbuilders but, generally speaking, the work was undertaken in the railway workshops. The companies became so proficient at this work that (during the war) they were asked to undertake sub-contract body-building work for both the Government and large motor manufacturers. According to Edwin Pratt's record of Government-account railway work during World War I, there was a large number of railway workshops undertaking body-building, but the L&YR's Carriage & Wagon Department at Newton Heath was undoubtedly the most proficient. During World War I they produced hundreds of bodies for both the army and Leyland Motors; ironically many of these trucks with L&YR bodies were sold to railway companies all over Britain once the war had finally ended.

Top Right: *During World War I, the Karrier Motor Company struck up a mutually rewarding relationship with the L&YR, and this arrangement was to continue with the LMS after the Grouping. Typical of the early products being supplied by the company was RO 1499 (No. 1132B) seen at St.Pancras Goods.* S. Shelton Collection

Middle Right: *A slight improvement on the Karrier shown above, but still carrying a Midland-style cab. However, the solid wheels have been replaced with pneumatic tyres, which gave a smoother ride for UR 3972 (No. 1763B). A windscreen has also been provided on this CH5Y model.* S. Shelton Collection

Bottom Right: *As the 1920s progressed, so did the quality of the vehicles used by the LMS. Contrast, if you will, UR 6783 (1948-B) with RO 1499. Note the enclosed cab (based on the LNWR design), which had a windscreen and doors and thus gave far greater driver comfort.* S. Shelton Collection

TRAMWAYS

This section is by no means a comprehensive account of the company's involvement in tramway operations, but it does serve as an indicator of the varied nature of LMS road vehicle operation. Two tramway systems were owned and operated by the LMS, these being the former LNWR tramway at Wolverton & Stony Stratford, and the 'light railway' sponsored by the Midland Railway between Burton and Ashby. Both of these ventures were absorbed by the LMS at the Grouping of 1923, but neither were destined for long lives; the Wolverton system closing in May 1926, with the Burton & Ashby succumbing nine months later.

The Wolverton & Stony Stratford District Light Railway Co. Ltd. was incorporated in 1886, and provided a link from the LNWR main line at Wolverton Station to Stony Stratford, serving the Wolverton railway carriage works and Old Wolverton en-route. Stony Stratford had been an important staging point on the Roman road called Watling Street (now the A5), but it had later been bypassed by George Stephenson's London & Birmingham Railway.

The need to link the town to the railway became very important, especially after the LNWR built its works at nearby Wolverton. By 1880 hundreds of workmen were walking each day from the town to the works, but the only transport was a horse bus costing 6d (2.5p). Despite this, the early plans all failed and the first services along the 3ft 6in gauge line began on 17th May 1887. A 2-mile long extension from Stony Stratford to Deanshanger opened in May 1888, but it was never a very solvent operation and the company went into receivership in September 1889. In 1891 Samuel Leon formed a new company to work the Stony Stratford - Wolverton section. Money was always tight, and derailments on worn track frequent, so by the end of World War I closure seemed imminent. However in 1919, the LNWR halted closure by purchasing the line and undertaking improvements. Motor bus competition was taking its toll, and by 1923 there were more than a dozen buses offering competing services. Despite this, the tramway could well have struggled on for some time to come, but the General Strike of 1926 led to its final demise. When tramways staff failed to turn up for work on 4th May the LMS closed the tramway and it never re-opened.

Top Left: *Wolverton & Stony Stratford tram locomotive, built by Bagnall (works number 308) in 1921. Ordered by the LNWR it had a short life, as the system was closed by the LMS during the General Strike of May 1926. Accompanying the tram engine is one of the 1886-built 100-seat passenger cars produced for the original tramway company by the Midland Carriage & Wagon Co. The view is outside the Foresters Arms c1923-4.* D.D. Gladwin Collection

Top Right: *In full LNWR livery tram engine No.4 is seen with double-deck car No.2. This tram engine was built by Brush of Loughborough (works no. 308) in 1904 and passed into LNWR ownership in 1920.* D.D. Gladwin Collection

Middle Right: *This attractive view shows the Burton & Ashby depot at Midland Road, Swadlingcote, with the cars 18, 5, 14, 9 and 10 in residence. Car No.1 stands outside carrying advertisements for holidays in the Isle of Man.* British Railways courtesy D.D. Gladwin

Bottom Right: *Burton & Ashby car No.4, one of the first batch built by Brush of Loughborough in 1906.* D.D. Gladwin Collection

It was the influence of the Midland Railway that led to the formation of the Burton & Ashby Light Railway, a 3ft 6in electric tramway connecting Burton on Trent and Ashby de la Zouch. The genesis of this line was due to the fact that the Midland line between these two points was so busy with freight traffic, that local passenger services were something of an encumbrance. The tramway was constructed to integrate with the Midland lines and stations in the area, but in later years the inter-connection of trams and trains was probably more co-incidental than contrived. It was a relatively short-lived system, operating a mere 21 years between 1906 and 1927, but at its height there were trams every ten minutes in peak periods, a schedule that required no less than 17 trams in operation. A fleet of 20 double-deck cars were built by Brush Electrical of Loughborough, and each of these could carry 51 passengers. They were originally painted in a Crimson Lake (Midland Railway red) and white livery, and given ornate gilt lettering. But as the years progressed this was simplified, and the LMS inherited a system that was not only looking a little down at heel, but was actually a dying operation. Once again motor buses took their toll, as did improved railway services, so the possibility of renewal and replacement never really presented themselves on a lengthy tramway system that passed through large areas of rural countryside. In his book, *Britain's First Electric Trams* (also published by Trans-Pennine), tramway historian Dave Gladwin makes comment that one particular type of traffic regularly seen on the Burton & Ashby was that of courting couples. One section of the line, known as the switchback, gave such a rough ride as to throw passengers close together. In the days of Edwardian Britain, when any form of close or intimate contact between courting couples (no matter how innocent) was frowned upon in public places, the switchback gave a good excuse. Consequently, return journeys on the line were common at weekends and holidays.

BUS OPERATION

From the tramways operations of the LMS to motor bus operation, it is but a short hop, skip and a jump, and this now forms the next logical progression in the LMS road vehicle story. In a sense, what happened on the LMS with motor buses closely parallels what happened with the Great Western Railway. That story has already been told in Volume Four of this series, *GWR Road Vehicles*, but there are significant differences. From that publication, the reader will see that the GWR commenced bus services in 1903, operating a service between Helston and the Lizard. This was, in fact, their response to demands to create a light railway from the Cornish market town to the popular tourist destination on the coast. Obviously it was much cheaper to test market demand with a bus service rather than go to the heavy expenditure that the fixed route of a railway line would incur. As it happened, despite early set-backs the bus service was a great success, and no railway was ever built down to the Lizard.

Above: *This superb view well illustrates the early LMS bus operations, with an Albion PM28 chassis purchased for use on the Gourock Pullman services, which the company acquired in 1929. Like many of its contemporaries, CH 7930 (fleet no.215F) was fitted with a Derby-built body.* S. Shelton Collection

Elsewhere the GWR introduced bus services, to obviate the need for new lines, but other routes were opened up as a means of feeding existing lines or services. The progress on the GWR was swift and continuous, to the extent that a substantial bus fleet had been built up on the eve of World War I. During the Great War the GWR not only introduced cut-backs in response to Government requests for economies, but they also suffered unfair competition from one-man operators who saw an opportunity and exploited it. Even so, by 1919 the railway were back in full swing, and bus operations formed an important element of their road motor vehicle operation. This continued down through the Grouping, and by 1922-3, the GWR had begun placing substantial orders to build up the fleet.

Top Right: *At an early stage, the railways realised the benefits of operating integrated feeder services. In the absence of one terminal station for central London, several of the pre-grouped companies provided interconnecting bus services. This pair-horse bus connected the Midland (St. Pancras) with the South Eastern & Chatham (Charing Cross) and the London & South Western (Waterloo).*

Middle Right: *Horse-buses continued the cross-London service for many years, but the railways were very keen to experiment with other forms of traction. With a passenger saloon not dissimilar to the horse-bus shown above, this Thornycroft was registered AA 887.*

Bottom Right: *The Midland operated buses not only in big cities, but in smaller towns and villages as well. This Wolseley (BD 717) provided a service at Rothwell near Leeds.* all S. Shelton Collection

The advantage that the GWR had over the other members of the Big Four was that it got off to a flying start by virtue of the fact that it had continuity of management. Nowhere was this more clearly demonstrated than in the GWR's bus operations which, by 1922, the company saw as being an important means of extending the carrying capacity of their railways into the surrounding hinterland. The fact that the railways had no legal powers to operate road bus services did not really deter them, as the GWR saw the buses as simply being a means to an end. In other words, like the road haulage of parcels and freight, it was simply viewed as being a part of an integrated service to the customer and end user. If the thing made a profit, it was all fine and dandy, but that was not the be all and end all of the matter.

Many constituents of other Big Four companies had adopted similar policies, and several of these had not only begun road freight services but had dabbled in bus operations also. Within the LMS constituent companies, the Caledonian, Furness, Glasgow & South Western, Lancashire & Yorkshire, London & North Western, Midland and North Staffordshire had all operated motor omnibuses, and other railways had owned horse buses as well. However, the advent of World War I and other problems of the period had seen the constituents gradually shedding their motor bus operations, and at the time of the Grouping on 1st January 1923, only two LNWR routes remained. Both of these were based on the town of Harpenden, with one running to Tring and the other to Hemel Hempstead and Boxmoor. This service utilised a fleet of five buses, although a sixth (ordered by the LNWR) was to be delivered shortly after the Grouping. These six buses were all bodied at the Wolverton Carriage Works, and were based on three Thornycroft J Type chassis and three Daimlers. A pioneering fleet, but hardly a major one! No further public service vehicles were ordered by the LMS until February 1928, when a Leyland PLSC3 with LMS bodywork entered service. More Leyland chassis were obtained towards the end of 1928, and between December of that year and December 1930, 62 more buses entered service. The chassis used were Leyland PLSC3 and TS2, AEC Reliance and Regal, Albion PNC, PR and PM and one Karrier Chaser which was fitted with a Craven body and used as a 'ro-rail' bus.

Top Left: *At the formation of the LMS, only a small number of buses were absorbed from the pre-group companies, and all of these were based in Hertfordshire. Here we see NK 2832 a 32-seat Thornycroft J-Type at Tring.* S. Shelton Collection

Middle Left: *The bulk of the LMS bus purchases came in 1929, when batches of Leyland, AEC, and Albion chassis were acquired. Leyland TS2 (UR 3764) entered service in June that year, and was fitted with a United C26F body. It later went to Hebble Motor Services in Halifax, along with UR 3765, a Cravens-bodied TS2.* S. Shelton Collection

Bottom Left: *Entering service on 1st August 1929, this Albion PM 28 with a Derby-built 32-seat was used to replace one of the ex-LNWR Thornycrofts on the Boxmoor, Hemel Hempstead, Harpenden service.* S. Shelton Collection

Although the LMS had developed a big road vehicle fleet by 1930, it represented only a fraction of what it could have done had it put its mind to it. The trouble is that there seems to have been dissension amongst senior management surrounding the whole issue of road motor operation in general, but with buses in particular being the main sticking point. Yet, unlike the GWR who seemed willing to skirt the issues of legality on bus service operations, the LMS waited until it actually gained an Act 'empowering the Company to provide, own, work and use road vehicles to convey by road, passengers and passengers luggage, parcels and merchandise, or to enter into agreement with any local authority, company, body or person owning or running road vehicles for hire or as a public service vehicle for the carriage of passengers, parcels or merchandise.'

Now the above Act did not come into being until 1928, the earlier Railway Road Powers Bill of 1924 having failed in its passage through Parliament. But, during this four year gap, had the private road transport operators (freight or passenger) sat back and waited for the outcome? Of course they hadn't, and these operators who had neither the desire nor the legal requirement to ask Parliament if they could begin a service, had certainly made inroads into the company's prime territory. These private operators, usually one-man concerns, had no qualms about taking away any traffic they could find, and they did so with frightening rapidity. It was in this period that the powerful road lobby had its origins, and this would have its own repercussions in the late 1950s when the twin transport reports of Beeching and Buchannan were ordered by a Conservative government, keen to abolish the power of the Triple Alliance (rail, coal and steel workers unions). Many of the haulage companies set up in those days obtained their business by undertaking jobs that were unreasonable by either ethics or good working practice. Several firms (just to keep their heads above water) willingly acted as 'strike breakers' in the 1926 General Strike, whilst others would drive long distances non-stop to compete with existing railway services. Sadly the roads and the lorries of the day were simply not up to the job, and several tragedies resulted as a consequence of drivers working excessive hours in poor conditions.

This is not to suggest that the majority of firms did anything dishonest, it was merely working to suit the conditions of the day. However, if firms tried anything like this today, the authorities would soon have them off the road. What is sad, is the fact that rather than working with the railways, and the railways working with the small hauliers (as they had done in the days of horse and cart), they each chose conflicting positions. Thus the chance of developing an integrated and comprehensive road-rail network foundered, as each sector chose to exploit some areas and neglect others. The market became fragmented, and eventually reliance would be placed upon private motor vehicles rather than public transport. Perhaps this will change one day and we will have a system of buses and trains working hand in hand, but we had the chance three-quarters of a century ago, and we squandered it completely.

That said, by 1929 the LMS were just poised to become a major bus operator in their own right, when a remarkable U-turn occurred. But first we must record just how the LMS were to expand into bus operations in a big way, by showing their acquisition of the following bus companies:- Ayrshire Pullman Co., Brookes of Rhyl, Crossville Motors, East Midlands Motor Services, Gourock Pullman Services, Holyhead Motor Co., Inverness Motor Service, and UNU Motors of Llangefni - some of which were jointly acquired with other railway companies.

The largest operation was of course the Crossville Company, which ran in North Wales, Cheshire and Merseyside. This was a real gem, and soon LMS Crossville began buying out competitors within its area of operation. A glance at a public transport map of the area between the Dee and Holyhead will show just how much of a monopoly the LMS enjoyed in early 1930. Yet in reality the LMS had paid over the odds for its bus operation acquisitions, and within a year things were to change. It has been commented that the LMS burned their fingers with Crossville, and thereafter preferred to enter joint ownership/working arrangements with other companies or operators. This could well be true, for future practice demonstrated that this would be the chosen course thereafter.

Top Right: *In order to expand its services in Scotland, the LMS purchased a number of small bus operators, and then began to build up the fleets. To undertake tour work from Oban, the company purchased this Albion PNC 26 and gave it a 26-seat coach body by Beatonsons. Note the canvas roof, which would be pulled back on sunny days to provide an open-top saloon. S. Shelton Collection*

Middle Right: *Another variation of a sun-saloon is seen on UR 6298, an Albion Viking Six with a 23-seat body by Watsons of Lowestoft. It was allocated to the Crossville fleet as No.411. S. Shelton Collection*

Bottom Right: *Purchased in 1929, when the LMS were the sole owners of Crossville Motor Services, FM 5749 was a Leyland TD1. With the LMS Crossville fleet number of 367, it was painted Crimson Lake with white bands and a grey roof. S. Shelton Collection*

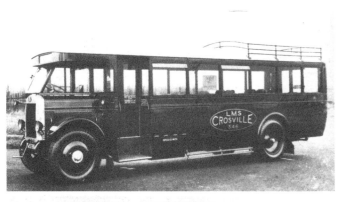

Top & Middle Left: *Strangely, whilst the LMS did not place many orders with Leyland Motors for commercial vehicle chassis, it did purchase quite a few bus chassis, mainly of the types PLSC3, TD1 and TS2. This reflected Leyland's growing dominance of the bus market at that time, and the purchases made by the LMS confirmed this. These two views of Leyland Tiger FM 5790 (Crossville fleet number 346), show it in Crimson Lake livery, with a grey roof and a crimson waist band, the lettering would have been in gold. LMS Official*

Bottom Left: *Having badly burnt their fingers with the Crossville acquisition, the LMS looked at safer ventures, and experimented with a number of joint undertakings with municipal authorities in the West Riding of Yorkshire. Here we see Huddersfield Joint Omnibus Committee's No.107. This Karrier's lower panel was Crimson Lake, the bands were off-white, and the upper panels red. LMS Official*

On 30th April, the LMS undertook to sell 50% of its shareholding in Crossville to the Tilling and British Electric Traction operation. In turn this gave the LMS an increased shareholding in other Tilling/BET companies. Share participation led to the LMS becoming involved in Hebble Motor Services at Halifax and the East Midlands operation in which the LNER also owned shares. Later in 1930 they took shares in W. Alexander, Birmingham & Midland Motor Omnibus (Midland Red), Cumberland Motor Services, Llandudno Coach & Carriage, Eastern Counties, Highland Transport, Lincolnshire Road Car, North Western Road Car, Ribble Motor Services, Trent Motor Traction, West Yorkshire Road Car, Yorkshire Traction and Yorkshire Woollen District.

With the LNER they took shares in the Scottish Motor Traction Co, W. Alexander, Greenock Motor Services, Macbraynes, Pitlochry Motors, and Rothesay Tramways (all in Scotland) and Eastern National in England. But perhaps the most interesting step was in the development of working arrangements with four municipal bus undertakings in the old West Riding of Yorkshire. From North to South, these were Todmorden, Halifax, Huddersfield and Sheffield. In the case of Todmorden and Huddersfield, the LMS entered partnerships with the local authority concerned, but in Halifax and Sheffield the LNER entered the partnerships as well. In all four instances these bus operations became known as Joint Omnibus Committees.

The railway involvement did not completely oust the local authority influence, for the reality saw two types of bus service existing side by side. In my home town of Huddersfield, the buses serving the inner urban areas were generally operated by Huddersfield Corporation Passenger Transport, whilst those serving outer areas were the responsibility of the Huddersfield Joint Omnibus Committee. The liveries were different, some working practices were different, but all of these worked to a common advantage. Indeed, on the formation of the Huddersfield JOC on 16th May 1930, the LMS saw the opportunity to rationalise rail services in the area. Accordingly on 26th July 1930 it withdrew passenger trains from the circuitous ex-LNWR branch to Kirkburton and replaced them with a more direct bus service.

The LMS involvement in local authority bus services continued down to nationalisation in 1948, and went even further. In fact the Joint Omnibus Committees would last for a further 20 years, and after the formation of British Railways led to even further examples of integrated bus-rail working. Returning to Huddersfield, May 1949 saw the JOC taking over the working of passenger services to Meltham. This allowed closure of the branch passenger service, but the savings achieved allowed the introduction of a new bus service to Houses Hill (on the opposite side of the town) and an improvement on routes between the Colne and Holme valleys. This not only improved bus services through Meltham, but it gave connections to the main trans-pennine line and the branch line at Holmfirth.

In my experience I found that the JOCs worked well and I was sorry to see their demise in 1968, when the Transport Act of that year saw the transfer of BR's road vehicle operations into other organisations (see our book *British Railways Road Vehicles 1948-68*). At this time the JOC buses/services were absorbed in to full local authority control, and another forward-thinking example of integrated road and rail services succumbed to the puerile mentality of a Government that could see no further than trying to stem short-term losses. Talk about throwing the baby out with the bath water! Perhaps the best example of all the JOCs, was that serving the Steel City, Sheffield! This was a wonderful example of how rail and bus could work together, and for those unfamiliar with the story I would highly recommend the book *Sheffield Transport* by C. Hall (Transport Publishing Co.).

Yet, whether the LMS bus involvement was with JOCs, joint-share, or direct ownership, I think that there is a moral in the story. Some people would say that improvement in any service only comes with true market competition, others would say that only by co-operation can you offer the best service to your end user. The concept of integrated road-rail interchange was certainly very much in the minds of the Big Four railway companies, and given the chance we might have developed interconnecting services like the Swiss developed theirs. However, that was not the case, and I leave it for the reader to judge who have fared better, British travellers or Swiss!

Top Right: *With a body by local builders, Cravens, this Sheffield JOC double-decker was part of the city's B Fleet. Still carrying trade plates, this Leyland is seen around the time of delivery. The livery here would have been dark blue and a cream-white with very ornate lining. As will be seen from the side panelling, the LMS were joined by the LNER in this joint omnibus arrangement.* LMS Official

Middle and Bottom Right: *It should not be forgotten that, in addition to service buses, the LMS owned a sizeable fleet of internal use vehicles. These buses were mostly associated with the Motive Power Department, where they were used as 'calling up' vehicles. This Bedford OB with a Duple service bus body dates from 1946, and was used by the Saltley Depot in Birmingham to collect staff at the start of their shift and drop them back home again afterwards. Registered GRO 206 it was fleet number 325S.* LMS Official

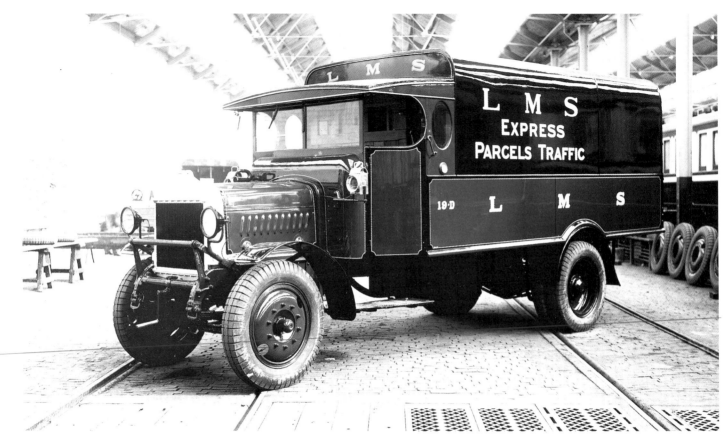

EXPRESS PARCELS VEHICLES

Those readers who have already read the two earlier railway road vehicle books in the Nostalgia Road series will understand how important Express Parcels Traffic was. In the scheme of things, this was the railway's premier service, and used by the general public and businesses alike. The LMS were the largest movers of Express Parcels! Their service was second to none in Britain and probably unrivalled anywhere else in the world. Not only were express consignments accepted at any railway station on the LMS system, but they could also be handed in at a vast number of agencies. These agents might be anything from rural post offices to city centre tobacconists or newsagents, or any commercial premises that were already served by one of the company's cartage or parcels routes. After thorough vetting of a prospective agent, a sign would be erected outside their premises and business commenced. The level of service operated by the Express Parcels network was one that many private couriers of today would be completely envious of, yet the LMS were doing this 75 years ago and no-one thought it remarkable!

Above: *Although quite a heavy chassis for Express Parcels work, this AEC Y-Type looks resplendent as it nears completion inside the Wolverton Carriage Works. It must be early in the LMS era, as the carriages behind are all still in LNWR livery.* LMS Official

Today firms like TNT, Securicor-Omega, Lynx and so on all offer a next day service, using network hubs to effect delivery within 24 hours. If truth is told the LMS did this before computerised manifests or automated proof of delivery systems, but generally urgent parcels could be moved from one end of the system to the other in less than 24-hours. What is more, and unlike the chaos that ensued in British Railway's days, the incidences of loss or delay were very minimal.

The LMS also had a cash on delivery service for their customers where, for a small commission, the railway would collect the money from the consignee and forward this to the sender. Collection values could be up to £100 (nowadays worth about £5,000), and payment was prompt. All of this aided cash flow and encouraged the customer to stay loyal to the LMS (if only our carriers could offer a service like that today *ed.*)

Top Right: *By way of contrast, we now show fleet number 308D, another Karrier, but this time one sporting the Midland Railway style cab. This cab is much cruder than the LNWR design, and offered little in the way of driver comfort.* S. Shelton collection.

Middle Right: *Slightly later than fleet number 19D shown opposite top, but once again carrying the LNWR Wolverton cab, we see 78D on a Karrier chassis. Mind you, although the paintwork on UR 7906 looks immaculate, you can notice bad 'runs' from the wheel discs down the sides of the Goodyear tyre walls. This particular van entered service in 1930, but this picture shows a re-paint date of September 1933.* LMS Official

Bottom Right: *Another Karrier, but one sporting the LMS Wolverton cab, is seen on 102D (JH 5396). This 3-ton van dates from 1931 and is pictured at Wolverton just after the completion of its body.* LMS Official

The origins of this type of parcels service are open to debate, and even amongst those who have made a comprehensive study of the subject there are differences as to where this type of service really began in an organised fashion. However, one thing that can not be denied is the fact that it was the Midland Railway who really made a go of the service. As we have already stated, the Midland really advanced their road-delivery and collection services in the last quarter of the 19th Century and had over 3,000 horse-vehicles by 1890.

Capacities and sizes of the horse-drawn express vehicles varied from constituent company to constituent company, and varied again within each individual company. Generally speaking the weights of the vans ranged from 12-cwt to 2½-tons. Usually these were all within the capability of a single horse, and for grounds of economy single horse working was the preferred arrangement. Some horse vans were fully covered, others were open vans with a canvas tilt. All the woodwork was generally finished in Crimson Lake, with the canvas painted black. The lettering could be either gilt or white. Depending on the areas where the horse vans would be operated, the wheels could be solid or pneumatic, and so the variations went on.

Each constituent company had its own preferences, some built 'economical' vehicles, which were cheap to construct but showed little longevity in service, others built substantially more durable vans albeit at an additional cost. However, on this point we might mention that a large number of Derby-built MR vehicles lasted well into BR days, and as such were some of the last horse-drawn road vehicles in use on the nationalised railway. There was some considerable rivalry between the Derby and Wolverton works when it came to building horse-drawn vehicles for the LMS, and in the early days of the newly formed company each of these works tried to better the other; but it was the Derby styling that was eventually adopted much to the chagrin of the ex-LNWR men. The huge variety of horse-drawn vehicles can not even be considered here, and we can only illustrate its wide variety with the few photographs shown on these pages.

Top Left: *Once again, another re-painted Express Parcels van, seen at Wolverton in October 1933. This features a Fordson B-Type JH 5510, LMS fleet number 434D.* LMS Official

Middle Left: *Another Fordson B is seen with UR 7759, fleet number 333D. This particular picture is one that should inspire modellers, for the clarity of the image is so good. The bulk of the body would have been Crimson Lake, and the goods compartment hood finished in gloss black. White lettering was used against the black background, whilst shaded gold lettering and lining was used on the Crimson Lake. The tyres were by Firestone.* LMS Official

Bottom Left: *Another type of light van used by the Express Parcel service was the 5cwt-7cwt Austin. Although not as numerous as the Fordsons, they were quite common. Here we see an Austin 10, JH 5728, occupying number 39D in the fleet list.* S. Shelton Collection

From the surviving evidence, it is obvious that there was some level of conflict between the former LNWR works and the former Midland works when it comes to road vehicles, and a degree of resentment that 'the powers that be' chose the Midland designs as standard. Durable they may have been, but they were far more utilitarian than those produced at Wolverton. This was quite an odd situation, for in almost every other sphere of railway vehicle building the Midland assumed a 'Rolls Royce' approach to building, whilst the LNWR were the 19th Century equivalent of Ford Motors. On the horse-drawn vehicles this difference was not all that noticeable, but when it came to road motor vehicles it was another matter altogether. To understand this the reader must appreciate that, in a large number of instances, the bodies applied to motor vehicles were nothing more than modified horse-vehicle designs. Consequently, as motor lorry and van chassis began to improve (often coming with stylish factory-built cabs), the railway-manufactured bodies looked angular and dated. It is said that the British Chevrolet company were in fact unwilling to sell their chassis cabs to the LMS, as 'the railway only added ugly boxes on the back!'

In the early days lorry manufacturers would simply sell a chassis to the LMS, and this would receive both a cab and body at either Derby or Wolverton. Like the more general delivery vehicles discussed later, the express van bodies could be unbolted from one chassis and put on another when required. The objective was to keep newer chassis for express traffic and cascade older ones to cartage and sundry work, but there is not that much evidence to support this as being regular working practice. However, the end result was a utilitarian box that was often ill-fitting and out of proportion to the rest of the vehicle. With only nominal alterations, one body style could be used on a Fordson B-Type or an AEC Y-Type. In October 1928 the LMS wisely decided to give road motor vehicle body design to the Wolverton Works, and an immediate improvement became evident. At once Wolverton adopted the later style of LNWR van body, but modified this to meet the needs of the era. One improvement was seen in the 'cab to body' access hatch provided for the van boys.

Yet the adoption of the LNWR styling for the Express Parcels vans was only a stop gap measure, and the second van style began to appear. This appeared on van chassis like the Morris Commercial and the Fordson, and provided a vehicle in the 30-35cwt range. A third style appeared by the mid-1930s and gave a less antiquated look, and a slightly longer goods compartment. The fourth style appeared just before World War II, with a van body being mounted on a lorry chassis, but left the cab and load-space as two separate units without a connection between them. In practice this made life difficult for the van boys, who now had to ride in the back of the van, or sort out consignments when the lorry stopped on its rounds. John McGarry recalled that they had an Austin at Gourock that was modified at the local workshops to provide an access hatch between the cab and the load space, but said 'the passage between the two compartments required you to not only be a contortionist but a limbo dancer at the same time!' Not only that, but the cutting of access panels also weakened the integral structure of the cab. In 1938-9 the LMS placed orders for a number of lorries (from Bedford, Austin and Rootes) to be supplied as 'chassis, cowl, screen and doors'. Photographic evidence suggests that the company then completed these units with their own roof panels and specially designed cab backs.

The Express Parcels vans featured a variety of chassis types. In the early 1920s, wartime chassis like Halley, Peerless, AEC and Leyland were supplemented by Model T Fords and Karrier 2-ton chassis. Over the years that followed the LMS demonstrated no particular loyalty to a single manufacturer and the list of types found in the Express Parcels fleet list is like a who's who of British commercial vehicle builders for it included:- AEC, Albion, Austin, Bedford, Commer, Dennis, Ford, Fordson, Karrier, Leyland, Morris and Thornycroft. However, of these makers Leyland only had a small representation, which was quite strange given the fact that they were based in what was entirely LMS territory. The accompanying pictures well demonstrate the tremendous variety in the LMS fleet, but it must have been something of a nightmare for the maintenance superintendent who had to carry suitable stocks of spares.

Top Right: *Pictured during World War II, this Fordson B-type carries fleet number 669D. Although painted in the joint livery of the LMS and LNER, BNK 598 was wholly owned by the LMS. Note that the van has been given a 'producer gas' conversion, and carries a special gas-bag rack on the roof. It has also had its leading edges and wheel arches picked out in white paint as part of the black-out precautions.* S. Shelton Collection

Middle Right: *One of the smartest of LMS Express Parcels vans was the 2-ton Dennis with the LMS Wolverton type 96 body. Here 703D shows off the combination to good effect.* S. Shelton Collection

Bottom Right: *Sister vehicle, 733D (BNK 778), is seen having a 'wash-down' at the end of a day's work, and bearing (appropriately enough) an advertisement for soap.* S. Shelton Collection

Sundries & Cartage Vehicles

In the movement of sundries and town cartage, the common distinguishing feature of horse-operation was the flat dray. These drays all looked very similar, and to the casual observer the only difference seemed to be whether the dray was pulled by one horse or two. But there were substantial differences and often drays were built for use in specific areas in order to meet the special requirements of the area in which they worked. For example drays that worked in the Yorkshire woollen districts were completely different to those that worked in Sheffield a few miles to the south.

Those that worked in country areas might have no seat, whilst those that worked in city centres were provided with a high seat in order for the driver to have a better view over the traffic and so on. Some drays were fitted with headboards, some were not, some had solid wheels with metal rims, others had pneumatic tyres and wheels with taper roller bearings. The braking systems also varied widely, ranging from un-brake and crude wooden blocks to foot-pedal-operated Ferodo brakes. A common feature to many however, was the front hoop frame which gave support for a canvas tilt cover.

The following chart provides some indication of the types used :

Type	Capacity	Model	Size
ST21	2¼-ton	Single-Horse Trolley (London)	12ft x 6ft 6in
ST22	5-ton	Pair-Horse Trolley (London)	14ft x 5ft 6in
ST23	6-ton	Trolley	14ft x 6ft
ST24	5-ton	Pair-Horse Trolley (London)	12ft x 6ft 10in
ST30	4-ton	ex-Midland Trolley (Manchester)	13ft x 6ft
ST32	35-cwt	Trolley	11ft 4in x 5ft 4in
ST33	65-cwt	Trolley	12ft x 5ft 6in
ST42	65-cwt	Trolley (Leicester & Manchester)	12ft x 6ft
ST45	6-ton	Trolley (Liverpool)	14ft x 6ft 6in
ST79	6-ton	Trolley (London)	14ft x 6ft 6in
ST87	3¼-ton	Trolley	16ft x 6ft
ST88	3¼-ton	Trolley	16ft x 6ft
ST92	6-ton	Container Trolley	14ft 6in x 6ft
ST98	2½-ton	Trolley with lift-off body	size not shown
ST99	3¼-ton	Trolley (steel-welded)	variable x 6ft
ST102	4-ton	Trolley	13ft x 6ft
ST103	8-ton	Trolley	? x 6ft
ST104	6-ton	Trolley	14ft x 6ft

Top Left: *This superb illustration dates from September 1931 and shows a Morris Commercial (JH 5705) dropside lorry before its allocation to the sundries fleet. Note that the LMS lettering is repeated in smaller point size on the sides of the platform for those times when the dropsides were removed. This lorry was No. 100B, and spent much of its working life in the Nottingham area, although it worked as far afield as London and Scotland at times.* LMS Official

Top Right: *Fleet number 709B, registered UR 6780, was another AEC Y-Type, and fitted with an LNWR style cab. Note that it carries a demountable dray platform, which actually has the separate fleet number 4840.* LMS Official

Middle Right: *Another platform lorry with a demountable platform (5254) is this rare Tilling-Stevens normal control chassis with Wolverton bodywork. Given the fleet number 684B, this unusual lorry was registered JH 3226.* LMS Official

Bottom Right: *Seen after a re-paint in 1933, JH 5392 is an Albion 3-ton chassis with Wolverton bodywork and numbered 49S in the fleet. Improvements to the original lights have been undertaken and a vacuum wiper blade fitted, but it still has the bulb horn.* LMS Official

With such a wide variety of dray designs available to meet differing workloads, and substantial numbers in service, it should not be a surprise to state that the LMS had developed standard techniques for both manufacturing and repair. Indeed, significant sums of money had been invested in the fleet of drays, lorries and trolleys, to the extent that when mechanisation of the road haulage fleet came about, the LMS were very reluctant to abandon their existing stocks. This point will be discussed more fully in the next chapter! However many readers will be familiar with the Mechanical Horse concept that the LMS evolved in order to replace horse haulage, whilst at the same time retain use of the existing drays etc. What may be less well known is the fact that the horse dray body also became the standard platform for road motor vehicles as well.

In the preceding chapter we have discussed how the LMS predominantly purchased commercial vehicle chassis and then bodied these to suit their own requirements for parcels traffic, and the same practice was true with regard to the motor lorries used on sundries and town cartage duties. Once again the duties of the vehicles within a given area or district would determine the types of platform mounted on the chassis, and as a general rule it can be stated that the motor lorries basically emulated the horse-drawn vehicles that had preceded them. The general purpose truck bodies that were built, depending on type, were constructed along the lines of the horse-dray with two main runners supporting transverse cross-members and deck planking. The whole platform was basically an independent unit, which (in turn) was fixed to a lorry chassis simply by means of a few 'U bolts'. This allowed for easy replacement and/or exchange, which in turn could be carried out in any depot where a crane was located.

Top Left: *Again with a Wolverton cab, we see an AEC Y-Type in the guise of UR 8883 (fleet number 877B). It has a demountable dray platform 5016. Its load on this occasion is one of the new standard railway containers based on the LMS B-type. These containers could fit equally on the back of a rail wagon, a horse-drawn dray or a motor lorry.*

Middle Left: *This B-Type container, employed in express furniture removal work, is seen on the back of this Midland-cabbed Karrier (fleet number 1754B). As the furniture removal men get to work with the sofa, this picture demonstrates the effectiveness of the service.*

Bottom Left: *Another type of container traffic is seen with these 2-ton H-Types loaded on to an AEC Y-Type JH 2937 at the former Cheshire Lines Committee station at Baguley.* All S. Shelton Collection

The types of lorry used to carry these platforms varied considerably, and once again the LMS does not seem to have used any one particular supplier over another. The AEC Y-Type was an early favourite though, and with bodies being built at both Wolverton and Derby, there are some interesting variations in the 5-ton range of vehicles. Albion was another popular make, and a number of these carried bodies manufactured by the ex-Lancashire & Yorkshire Railway carriage works at Newton Heath. Indeed, the LMS purchased quite a number of ex-War Department Leylands and Albions from the Government, the majority of which had been bodied at Newton Heath in 1918-1919 but seen little military use. Generally speaking Leyland Motors were an under-represented manufacturer in the LMS fleet, whereas Karrier Motors were favoured with quite large orders.

For the lighter types of commercial, Karrier and Ford both did very well, but following the Depression (and the Wall Street Crash) the LMS adopted a 'Buy British' campaign. Consequently Ford, Chevrolet, Dodge and British Chevrolet-Bedford (then owned by General Motors) all fared particularly badly. Morris Commercial, Dennis, Thornycroft and (to an extent) Austin all began to pick up business instead. There were some even more esoteric makes and the little Bradford firm, Jowett, received quite a few orders for light vans. Even the bus chassis manufacturers Tilling Stevens got some orders for commercial goods vehicle chassis. By the end of the 1930s it was something of a different story, and from then on until the end of 1947, the LMS found themselves lucky to be able to buy whatever commercial vehicle chassis it could.

Newcomers to the fleet in the period 1939-1947 witnessed some superb British lorries, including AEC Matador MkIIs, Bedford O and OWL, Austin K2, Dennis 30cwt or 40/45cwt and even an odd Maudslay Marathon or two. That is not to say that the older types did not linger on, as did the horse-drawn drays. In fact it was not until well into nationalisation that this wide, varied and increasingly antiquated fleet was modernised to meet the needs of the railway's customers. By the end of the 1940s it was sadly a moribund part of BR's inheritance, but at that time no-one had recognised the problem for what it truly was.

Given the concept that the railway road vehicle service had the objective of collecting traffic for the railway or dispersing it to the consignee, no-one had really thought through the true implications of the service. In 1939 the LMS did commission a report into its cartage operations, but its findings were overtaken by the outbreak of World War II and never acted upon. But this study had some interesting recommendations in that:

1. All horse vehicles should be withdrawn within a five year period.
2. Mechanical Horse operation should be up-rated to a standard 6-ton capacity.
3. Rural cartage and parcel delivery should be let to sub-contracting agents.
4. Network centres should be established for the movement of goods along the lines of the GWR zonal scheme.
5. Stronger lobbying should be made on the Government to ensure that the private road haulage industry does not gain unfair advantage in respect of the company's Common Carrier Obligation.
6. That the company be allowed to refuse traffics which it considers unreasonable to carry on the grounds of economy.
7. Where possible vehicle types be standardised on a smaller number of manufacturers

Undoubtedly this would have helped a rationalisation in the unwieldy road delivery operation, as would more stringent central control. As it was, the delivery vehicles at outlying stations and depots were very much operated on the whims of the individual Station-master or Goods Agent, and as will be seen in a later chapter this autocratic rulership did not always go down too well. Yet despite all this, it has to be said that the road motor operations did bring in a tremendous level of business for the LMS, and whatever it cost it could be described as a truly profitable loss-leader. What is more, during the dark years of World War II, it provided a service to the nation, in which both men and vehicles undertook valuable duties that will probably never be truly recognised nor fully appreciated.

Top Right: *A bit of a rare beast, this picture of UR 7913 shows a twin-rear axle Fordson A-Type. A batch of these trucks (UR 7900-7919) were purchased for a country lorry service, and were considered ideal for either light traffic or moderately heavy loads. Most of these were given Midland-style cabs at Derby, but UR 7919 was pictured with an LNWR style cab.* LMS Official

Middle Right: *A major development in LMS lorries came with the introduction of the Dennis 40/45cwt into the fleet, for here we had (for the first time) a lorry with a manufacturer's cab as opposed to one built by the railway. This one CNK 31, is seen at Sheffield's Wicker Goods Yard, carrying fleet number 2464B.* S. Shelton Collection

Bottom Right: *Another highly manoeuvrable lorry was the Bedford-Scammell OSS. Here we see an 8-ton tractor unit and 20ft. trailer shortly before delivery in 1946.* Scammell Lorries Ltd.

TRACTORS & TRAILERS

This chapter of the book occupies just a small section compared with its importance to the story, indeed one could write an entire book on the subject; in fact that is just what Bill Aldridge has already done, and in the companion **Nostalgia Road** title *Mechanical Horses*, the concept is fully discussed. Naturally, we hope that those interested in the story will purchase that particular volume, but we can not escape without mentioning what an important role the LMS played in the development of the articulated lorry - something which came about through the Mechanical Horse that was conceived by the LMS to meet the needs of the 1930s.

These needs came about due to a dark October day in 1929, after the world's economic stability took a massive blow when the American stock market crashed overnight. Almost instantly world trade was decimated, nothing had any real value anymore, and the world's shipping, railway and transportation companies found themselves at the very fulcrum of trade decline.

Above: *This picture of a Scammell tractor and trailer unit (UR6305 - 1931B) is representative of the company's first moves into articulation.* LMS Official

Now unlike a ship, steam engine or aeroplane that can be tied up, stabled or put in a hanger when there is no use for it, the same could not be said for the road haulage fleets of the day. The simple reason behind this statement is the fact that, despite much modernisation, over 60% of Britain's road freight was still being hauled by horses. In America it was 64% and some European countries had up to an 82% dependency on horse-haulage. Consequently, when the traffic dipped, the horses had to be stabled. Yet, despite the fact that they were not earning any income whatsoever, they still had to be fed and watered. Most companies would tolerate this situation for a while, but if went on for any prolonged period of time older beasts would be sold or culled. I do not propose to quote any figures for the number of horses slaughtered in the first half of 1930, but if you know where to look the statistics make tragic and unhappy reading.

Now, as the railways in general (and the LMS in particular) were the biggest owners of horses in Britain, it was obvious that a substantial fall in traffic would result in a shift policy regarding horse-operation. Indeed, as the effects of the Depression became more pronounced, the LMS decided it needed to radically reduce its horse stud. Now that is all well and good, but if you dispense with your horses, what do you do with the associated equipment and premises that you have operated with that stud. This thorny problem had been one with which the LMS had been wrestling since 1926, and had probably been the reason why they had decided not to widely implement motorisation of their road fleet at a much earlier stage. After all the company owned hundreds of stables and thousands of horse-drawn drays and vans, many of which had been built since the end of the Great War in 1918. Given that these drays and vans were less than 10-years into a projected 30-year life span, to simply discard them would have been economic madness.

Furthermore the buildings (like stables, warehouses and so on), which had been made to accommodate horse-drawn traffic, could not easily handle motorised vehicles with their greater width and larger turning circles. It was the same with the majority of the railway's customers, as their premises were primarily built to accept horse-drawn traffic and little else. Therefore, until increased capital expenditure could be justified, what was needed was a stop-gap or interim transport facility. In other words, the company needed something that had all the versatility of the horse, could enter buildings made for horses, and use existing horse-drawn equipment, yet (at the same time) not incur the standing costs associated with keeping live animals.

The answer was a Mechanical Horse which, like the horse and cart, was ideally suited for local delivery and collection work. The versatility of a vehicle that could swiftly couple or uncouple a trailer, and leave this to be loaded or unloaded (whilst it went off with another trailer) would also take the horse-drawn operation a stage further. Yet it was this basic concept that dramatically influenced the development of modern transport in the shape of the articulated vehicle.

Top Right: *The replacement of horse-drays by motor lorry was a real advantage, but the facility of stand drays that could be loaded or unloaded whilst the horse was away on its rounds, was a facility that had to be retained, so experiments were tried with demountable dray platforms. Here an AEC Y-Type (854B) transfers dray platform 5047 on to a stand dray.* LMS Official

Middle Right: *The next stage was the Mechanical Horse which could work with existing horse drays, here we see the prototype Karrier Cob (UR 9869 - fleet number1G) at work with horse-dray 15554. Note that the original front axle and wheels have been retained on the dray, which demonstrates that the initial concept behind this tractor was a mechanical replacement for the dray horse..* S. Shelton Collection

Bottom Right: *A more familiar sight is seen here with the 319th mechanical horse, a Scammell 6-tonner registered ANK 288, which is seen pulling a Dyson Trailer tanker off a rail wagon.* S. Shelton

Top Left: *No conflict between Scammell and Karrier? Here we see two LMS drivers shaking hands in front of their respective steeds at the 'Knights of the Road' awards. The one on the left has a 3-ton Scammell Mechanical Horse (ANK 360), whilst the other drives a 3-ton Karrier platform lorry (CH 5635).* S. Shelton Collection

Middle Left: *Not often seen in books on the LMS are the Latil tractors, despite the fact that the company had quite a large number of these units. This one, BNK 456 (2409B) was based at Edge Hill and moved heavy loads around Liverpool docks.* S. Shelton Collection

Bottom Left: *The Dennis 40/45cwt rigid lorry, with its relatively short wheelbase proved to be highly manoeuvrable in railway goods yards, and the LMS decided to experiment with a tractor unit to form a 6-ton Mechanical Horse. This is shown to good effect with this view of GAR 65 (2729BG).* Bill Aldridge Collection

There had been a variety of experiments with tractors and trailers since the early days of railway road vehicle operation, with the 5th-wheel concept being a tried and tested method. Other experiments with demountable bodies, movable dray platforms and so on had all been tried, but by the mid-1920s there was no startling development that jumped up and shouted 'use me instead of the horse and cart'. But one did have more merit than the others, having been devised by the L&YR and later adopted by the LNWR. This was a demountable dray platform which was carried by rollers onto or off of a rigid motor lorry body. The lorry would back into a loading bay, the dray would be rolled off for loading or unloading as the case maybe, whilst the lorry went off with another dray body. When the first dray platform had been dealt with on the loading bay, it could be put on to another lorry or kept on a horse dray until such time as the original lorry returned to collect it. This system saved nothing in loading or unloading time, but it did free up the motor vehicle to make another collection or delivery.

On the formation of the LMS this system was retained at those depots where it already existed, but the company decided to adopt a better method of goods handling than extend this system across the network. The GWR were already experimenting with the 5th-wheel when the LMS decided to convert a Morris car chassis to pull a horse dray. They reasoned 'why go for complicated dray transfer from motor lorry to motor lorry, if you could develop some sort of mechanical tug that could be used to pull the existing horse drays'. Indeed, by allocating two or three drays to each 'tug', the same reduction in driver waiting time could be achieved and no added expenditure need be incurred in developing new systems. So, having decided on the development of a tug or 'mechanical horse' the LMS persisted in its quest. The sticking points were two-fold, as the Morris was obviously too light for the job, and secondly (and more importantly), the coupling of trailers was slow and cumbersome; in practice it required a couple of screw-jacks to achieve the coupling of the trailer to the car. It was therefore decided to drop the Morris and replace it with a Roberts platform truck and this proved to be a quite successful combination.

Now whilst the concept had started to move forward, the Roberts truck was not considered suitable for a large-scale application and as a consequence the LMS approached Karrier Motors to build something a little more robust. The Yorkshiremen responded with a will and made a modified version of their small 3-wheel dustcart chassis known as the Colt which gave positive indications. A prototype 3-wheel ''tug' was then built and sent to Wolverton for testing with modified horse drays. It was later given the fleet number 1G, and sent back to Yorkshire where it worked in Halifax. Fortunately this vehicle (seen on the rear cover) was later preserved and it can be seen at the National Railway Museum in York. The tug, later known as a Karrier Cob, coupled up to a horse dray with the shafts removed. The tug connected to the dray by means of a hand-operated hydraulic coupling, which engaged an axle beam on the dray and thus lifted the wheels on that axle from the ground.

It was not a wholly ideal solution, and within a few weeks an order had been passed that did away with the mandatory ruling that horse-drays had to be used without any modification. This allowed the engineers at Wolverton to strip off the front axle from the dray, and in its stead mount a set of landing legs between which the tug's rear axle would fit. This design was progressively modified in the weeks ahead, and soon it was developed into an automatic coupling system that would allow easy coupling between the tractor unit and the trailer. To couple it was simply a matter of backing on to the trailer, whilst uncoupling was achieved simply by releasing a latch in the cab which, in turn, activated a mechanical linkage with the trailer. This coupling device was further refined by both Karrier and the LMS, with the former version remaining in production until the 1950s. A little later a new 3-wheel tug built by Scammell, called The Mechanical Horse, featured a fully automatic trailer coupling and this was to become the standard fitment for all the British railway companies. The original Cob model was soon updated by Karrier and given a coupling that was compatible with the Scammell fitting. The Scammell tractor remained in production until 1948, and were then superseded by the Scarab. Karrier's 3-wheeler was never as popular with the railways, especially after 1936 when the 4-wheel Karrier Bantam tractor was introduced.

Top Right: *In 1938 the LMS began to experiment with a Bedford-Scammell combination. Although this particular model has a look of the OSS, it is in fact a WT series truck with the new Willenhall Radiator Company bonnet and radiator grill pressings. The trailer (1704GT) was obviously LMS stock but the tractor was merely a Bedford demonstrator.* Brian Madeley Collection

Middle Right: *Conversely, GAR 279 (2725BG) was an LMS unit, this time an OWS (O-Type, war-time, Scammell). With its utilitarian tin front it is seen at the Watford factory c1941.* Brian Madeley Collection

Bottom Right: *This time we see the post-war version, a Bedford OSS 8-ton tractor unit. Here GRO 285 (3331BG) is about to couple up on to a Dyson trailer during tests at Euston in 1947. The concrete block on the Scammell coupling is to give extra adhesion.* Vauxhall Motors

SPECIAL VEHICLES

In any sizeable transport organisation, it is inevitable that a fleet of miscellaneous vehicles will be developed in order to handle special types of traffic. Given that the LMS were common carriers, this fleet of special vehicles included some unusual pieces of equipment designed to handle unusual types of traffic. Bearing in mind that other hauliers could not (or would not) handle some of these unusual types of traffic, it fell upon the railways to move it, even though it may have been uneconomical to do so. In itself the rate charged for the job might have been profitable, but it was often the need for extra handling equipment that turned the profit to a loss. That is not to say that the railways had to purchase special equipment every time, obviously it did not, but even if equipment was used for several consignments, it would take a long time to pay off its capital costs. When the equipment was used to move loads in a wider area, there was an additional expenditure incurred in moving it from goods yard to goods yard.

Above: *This superb picture well illustrates the LMS special vehicle fleet, as a Walker-Pagefield crane is captured during acceptance trials. Still carrying trade plates 083 JH, the 6-ton crane lifts a baling machine on to horse dray 7886. Note the swivel seat that enables the driver to operate the crane.* LMS Official

A typical example might be a mobile crane which, whilst being useful in a number of differing tasks, had a high acquisition cost. The crane would be based at a central depot, as for example two Walker cranes allocated to Chester. These cranes would not only be used in that city, but could equally be employed as far away as Holyhead on Anglesey. With a top road speed of 15mph and a fuel consumption of 9mpg, taking a mobile crane more than a few miles became an expensive exercise.

However, mobile cranes well illustrate the need for special equipment, as it was found that such vehicles would provide an integral part of the road motor service, especially after the 'Big Four' railways introduced the standard railway container system in 1928.

At stations and goods yards where larger capacity yard cranes existed, and at factories (or other commercial premises) that had their own lifting equipment, there was no problem in handling the new containers. They fitted on a standard rail wagon and could be transported by road on either a horse dray, mechanical horse or a rigid platform lorry, so they were an ideal medium for many applications. The beauty of the system was that an empty container could be left at a factory, loaded by the staff there, and then sent direct to their customer who would use his own staff to accomplish unloading. It was secure, safe and reasonably efficient, but it was only practical where the sender and consignee had the means to get the container on or off the road delivery vehicle. There were further difficulties at those stations where the goods crane was in the warehouse, or where it was of a smaller capacity than the containers being handled. The only apparent answer was the use of block and tackle, or was it?

As a result of the Depression, a Lancashire firm of commercial vehicle builders, Walker Bros of Wigan were desperately seeking new work, and in a chance conversation with Harold Davies of the LMS, Walker's discovered the problem of handling containers. Walker offered to build a mobile crane for the LMS, and early in 1929 a Monitor Mobile Crane was evaluated at St. Pancras Goods Depot. This vehicle had a Dorman engine with a chain-drive to the rear axle, and generator-powered electric motor for the crane. It weighed 18-tons and had a lifting capacity of 6-tons. The LMS Directors were impressed, for not only could this crane be used in goods yards, but it could also be employed at the customers' premises if they did not have adequate lifting capacity. As a consequence, it was not unusual to see a wagon or mechanical horse carrying a container being followed down the road by a mobile crane as both proceeded to the consignments final destination. Convoluted it may have been, but it really did provide a true door to door service. Over the years cranage improved considerably, as did other handling techniques, but we should point out that the LMS also introduced a light crane on the back of some of their platform wagons for handling small loads. Modern drivers please note, HIAB units are not a new concept.

Top Right: *Behind the 3-ton Scammell Mechanical Horses, ANK 695 (653G) a Booths crane is pictured at Stoke in 1936 as it loads a B-Type container on to the Mechanical Horse trailer. This crane was very short-lived in LMS stock, and the only one of its kind, but no other picture is known to exist.* S. Shelton Collection

Middle Right: *It was not unknown for the pre-grouped companies to experiment with special vehicles, and in order to tow horse drays loaded with heavy bales of cotton, the L&YR invested in this International tractor with rubber studded wheels.* LMS Official

Bottom Right: *To enable ordinary lorries in the fleet to carry unusual loads, the LMS bought several four-wheeled 'dolly trailers'. One of these is well illustrated here with AEC Y-Type (UR 8658 - 759B), which is being used to move steel girders.* R. Fysh Collection

Top Left: *Fitted with a horsebox body by Vincents of Reading, this Leyland Cub was a rare member of the fleet. In fact it is a bus chassis, which was used to give a low-loading height essential for the high quality animals moved by the LMS 'Horse Transport Service'. The bulk of horses moved by fleet number 500D would have been racehorses, hunters and the like.* Leyland Motors, courtesy S. Shelton

Middle Left: *Still on its trade plates, this Albion M35 is seen shortly after delivery in December 1929. It is fitted with a two-tier sheep transporter body and an ingenious tail-board arrangement. Registered UR 4948 it became fleet number 1818B.* S. Shelton Collection

Bottom Left: *For the movement of other livestock, mainly cattle, the workshops at Derby built this type of body. Fitting it to the Fordson A-Type chassis, with twin rear axles, made it a light, go-anywhere vehicle, and a very useful member of the fleet. This one was JH 4983 with fleet number 605B.* R. Fysh Collection

Whilst mobile cranes are a good example of the railway's special equipment and special vehicles, they represent only a small fraction of the whole equation. Obviously the equipment used for handling seasonal or special traffic resulted in the accumulation of a large number of vehicles, in this regard we could cite those employed with the seasonal movement of agricultural produce, or those used to move shows, fairs and circuses. Large and bulk loads required heavy haulage to facilitate movement between the sender and the originating railhead, and then again between the receiving railhead and the consignee.

Examples of this type might include steam boilers, generating plant, transformers and so on. Where such equipment was originated there was no particular problem with the road haulage side of the operation, as this formed a regular traffic and there would be suitable road vehicles available within the district. However, it was often a major problem at the receiving station as, within certain districts, this type of traffic was so sparse as to not justify the allocation of special vehicles to it. A very good example of this could be found in Scotland, where both the Highland and South-western areas were so sparsely populated as to require only the most basic facilities. Yet large, bulk loads did get consigned to such areas, and when they did, special vehicles would have to be brought in from the outside. On occassions it was even found expedient to move the road haulage vehicles to the receiving station in the same train conveying the goods.

By adopting a policy of centralising its special vehicle fleet at a small number of locations, the LMS found itself more ready to handle the special traffics than any of the other Big Four companies. It is arguable that they were the most proficient at handling special traffic, but the LMS carried by far the great amount of special goods traffic and it stands to reason that they would have sought the easiest and most economical means of handling it. The movement, by rail, of the associated handling equipment was later adopted by the LNER and to a lesser extent by the GWR, but I can find no record of it having been a common practice on the Southern Railway.

Now, having discussed special vehicles, special lifting equipment and the like, our attention must turn to ordinary vehicles used for special duties. In this we refer to services operated by the railway, which were (at first consideration) seemingly outside normal railway operations. Obviously vehicles used by the Civil Engineer's Department, Advertising Department, Signalling & Telegraph Department and Chief Mechanical Engineers Department had a logical existence. These fleets were quite large and really form part of another book, but they included standard cars, vans and lorries as well as more esoteric vehicles used for special duties. But how many people would take you seriously if you told them that the LMS had fire engines, ambulances and police cars. Yet you would be perfectly correct in saying this, as the road motor fleet reflected the many and varied activities carried out by the company.

There were laundry vans, mobile canteens, hotel delivery vans, steamship tenders, station platform trucks, dung and manure trucks, mobile conveyors, stone lorries, tipper trucks, refuse vehicles, bullion trucks (armoured vans), printers vans, and a whole host of others too numerous to mention. As the company developed its road motor department, it became quickly aware of the potential in mechanising as many aspects of its non-railway transport activities as it could. That is not to say that it was done at any cost, quite the reverse for the acquisitions always tended to be the more frugal types of vehicle. A good example of this frugality is shown in the 'Goods Agent's' car at Derby works. This vehicle was based on an Austin 10/4 and had two front passenger seats, the rear portion however was converted to a load-space area and designed to be used for the movement of goods whilst the agent was on his rounds.

Yet there could be no doubt about it, the LMS had discovered the benefit of moving on from the horse, and in every area of operation (with perhaps the exception of town cartage) a progressive motorisation policy was adopted throughout the 1930s. It was to prove to be a very fortunate policy, as the coming years of trouble between 1939 and 1945 would clearly show!

Top Right: *As stated earlier, the LMS bought a number of vehicles straight off the peg, so to speak, including a number of Austin Sevens and Austin Tens and then put them straight into service with little or no modification. This Austin Seven JH 5727 was used by the Advertising Department, and would have been seen at many locations putting up posters and distributing leaflets. A possible idea for a model railway scene perhaps?* S. Shelton Collection

Middle Right: *Another unusual Austin is this 10/4 purchased for use by Goods Agents in Scotland. It has a pair of seats in the front, whilst the rear seats have been stripped out and turned into a goods-carrying compartment capable of carrying 1-ton.* LMS Official

Bottom Right: *For use at engineering works, docks etc., the LMS had their own fire brigades. Here the Crewe works fire engines are seen with the fire train. These are a Dennis New World (CNK 496) and a Fordson 7V (GAR 333).* R. Fysh Collection.

LIFE IN THE ROAD MOTOR DEPARTMENT

To give a little flavour to this narrative, we interviewed four former employees with the road motor department, commencing with P. Stoneman who recorded. 'I joined the Road Motor Department of the LMS Railway Company at the age of fourteen in August 1941. I was employed in Northampton, where the workshop, office and stores were in converted stable buildings in the Far Cotton Goods Yard. The staff was small, one leading fitter, one first class fitter, one third class fitter, one labourer and myself. This depot was classed as an 'out station' and the work was mostly servicing and repairs. The vehicle fleet at Northampton consisted of private cars, heavy and light lorries and Scammell Mechanical Horses, but no Karrier Cobs. In fact during the 16 years I worked in the RMD I never saw a Cob but I have a photo of one working in Northampton. This must have been replaced when the new Scammell's were put into service. As a pre-war school boy I had a collection of Hornby trains and Dinky toys and my father wanted to buy me the LMS model of the Karrier Cob but I did not like it, saying 'it's not like our Scammell Mechanical Horses'.

During 1943 we took delivery of four brand new Wilson Electrical Scammell's in place of four petrol MH3s. It was found that because of the extra weight of the batteries they were hard to steer at slow speeds, so the steering wheels were changed for the larger diameter MH6 type steering wheels to give more leverage. After a short time in service several electric motors burnt out, thought to be caused by stalling on inclines with a full load. As the motors cost £50 each (a fortune compared to my week's wage of 12/6 - 62.5p) it was decided to fit a heavy-duty overload relay in the main circuit of each vehicle. An electrician came from the LMS works at Stonebridge Park, London, and I helped him fit these relays and alter the wiring. This modification cured the problem. On these Wilson Electric Scammell's the controls for operating the vehicle were:-

1. Key and push switch to set relay;
2. Forward - off - and reverse switch;
3. Foot pedal to adjust speed.

The foot pedal was the old clutch pedal using the left foot. After being used to pressing down this pedal to select a gear in petrol MHs, it came as a shock when using this pedal on the Wilson, as the driver suddenly shot forward or backwards.

Top Left: *This trio of pictures shows the problems faced by the LMS with regard to goods handling. Firstly, THE DAILY SHUFFLE, reflects the desire to utilise stand trailers whilst delivery wagons were on their rounds, and epitomises the railway's struggle with pre-conceived ideas. These ideas dogged the railways right down until 1968, when the answer had been devised by the LNWR back in the 1880s. The now common wheeled cage could have been the answer all along, but as this picture shows, the idea of complete body/platform transfer was ever at the front of their minds.* R. Fysh Collection

Top Right: *Then we have THE DAILY PROCESSION, well illustrated as lorries left /arrived at the depot all at the same time. Here we see a line-up of ten vehicles leave Camden Goods Depot headed by AEC Y-Type NK 2914 in 1934.* S. Shelton Collection

Bottom Right: *Then comes THE DAILY TOIL, with the goods being manhandled up to five or six times from their coming off a train to their final delivery. Had a cage/basket system been implemented, then handling would have been substantially reduced. As it is William T. Garrard (driver) has to lift down a heavy parcel from his van boy (his wife, Violet May). This picture was taken on 24th February 1941 and shows a Mechanical Horse based at Euston.* LMS Official

Regular drivers soon got used to this pedal control but casual drivers and fitters sometimes fell into a trap. Mind you, I could never understand why the electric power for the lights and windscreen wiper on these vehicles was supplied by a separate 6-volt battery. This of course had to be exchanged when flat.

As Northampton depot was classed as an 'out station', under the terms of my apprenticeship I had to spend two years in a main workshop. I was most fortunate in that the engine and chassis section of the road motor workshop at Kentish Town, London, had been evacuated to Wolverton works due to the bombing. So I spent two happy and informative years with fitters overhauling Scammell, Dennis and Gardner engines. On my return to Northampton I carried on to the end of my apprenticeship, working on petrol, electric and diesel vehicles, also engineers plant, cranes, compressors and welding machines. On becoming a fitter 1st-Class I had my own group of vehicles to service and I still have some vehicle hand books that I used during this period.

With the threat of invasion during World War II, the Government ordered that all motor vehicles (when not in use) had to be immobilised. With our railway vehicles this was difficult, as none had door locks and some did not even have doors. It was also impossible for the rotors to be removed from magnetos by the drivers, so the drivers were instructed to remove the sparking plugs at the end of their shift. These were then placed in large OXO tins, with the vehicle numbers painted on them, and hidden in the mess room. This was not a great success owing to plug terminals dropping into cylinders and drivers mixing up ignition wires. To overcome this all vehicles were fitted with a heavy chain and padlock with which the steering wheel was locked to a staple on the dash or door pillar.'

Above: *As an example of what life was like in a war-time LMS road vehicle depot, we show this picture of Bradford Croft Street in 1942. The incumbents at this time were Fordson ANK 974, Karrier Cobs ANK 150/152, Morris Commercial lorry JH 7540, and Morris Commercial Van JH 5384.* Bill Aldridge Collection

Mr. Stoneman also recalls that; 'The petrol pump at the Castle Station goods yard had to be put out of action if the Germans landed. This pump was a hand operated semi-rotary type and I was sent on my bike to paint a red square on the face of the pump to indicate where it was to be broken with a hammer and cold chisel. It never had to be put out of use, and over the years I operated this pump to supply odd vehicles that called in for petrol, such as Pickfords, Hayes Wharf Cartage and other firms who had an arrangement with the LMS. Some of these large vehicles required 40-gallons and it was hard work pumping this amount. On the formation of British Rail we took over several LNER MHs, which were in poor condition, including a very early Scammell MH3. This vehicle still had the high ratio steering box and single pair of coupling hooks for the trailer coupling. I fitted a new engine and a low ratio steering box, and also a standard coupling hook.'

Robert Baddeley found himself working at Shap station in 1940, where he had been assigned as a warehouse boy working under the Goods Agent Mr. Morgan. He recalls, 'I arrived at Shap in the terrible winter, it having taken me some 18 hours to travel from Great Barr in Birmingham. I was just fifteen at the time and had never been further than the local zoo or the city centre before. Dad was a goods guard who worked out of Walsall, and he had once been to Shap in the 1930s, but all he could tell me was that it was on top of a mountain. I was to lodge with a signalman at a place called Thrimby, and in the first weeks at work I had to trudge through miles of snow to get to work for 7.30am. Only later did any one tell me how to get a lift on a passing train.

My duties mainly involved in parcels handling, but at this time we were getting a lot of kit bags and officers' trunks, all of which were sent to Lowther Castle as a new army training ground was being set up there. I never liked it much at Shap, and the goods agent didn't like me or the way I talked. However, as it happened, the Quartermaster at the army camp also came from Great Barr, and he took me under his wing so to speak, and after three months I was given the job of 'railway receiving clerk' and based in the estate office at Lowther not far from Thrimby.

This job meant that I was still working for the LMS, but under the direction of the army. They had people called RTOs in those days who co-ordinated railway movement for the military, and my RTO was a Mr. Howie who was a Major in the Southern Railway's Territorial Squad, and who had worked on ambulance trains in World War I. He worked from Victoria Station during peace time, where he was responsible for express parcels. I would learn more from him in the next 15 months than I would have learned from Mr. Morgan in a month of Sundays.

One of my main jobs was organising the movement of petrol to Lowther. As this was required in copious amounts, not only were we to use railway lorries, but we also used army trucks and two flat-bed Morris Commercials that the LMS hired from a local contractor. One of these Morris lorries was very badly maintained and its platform bed had so many holes in it that it looked like a colander. As the petrol was all to be moved in large jerry cans (we had no tanker wagons), the loads carried from Penrith Goods Yard to Lowther were very heavy. Therefore the engineers stripped off the old lorry platforms, and replaced them with a deck made up of railway sleepers.

I liked working at Penrith, it was a happy place, and it was a good team to boot. There were eight horse drivers, three motor drivers, and two drivers who could work either horses or road motors. We also had two or three ladies who worked as driver's assistants. The accompanying pictures show the 'team' in or around the summer of 1942. I would go from Lowther to Penrith at least once a day, and yet I would go to Lowther Station perhaps just once a week. The camp at Lowther, set up in the grounds of a magnificent castle that had been stripped of its roof and interior a few years earlier, was the scene of much secret testing. We had a lot of armoured vehicles coming to the camp, including some incredible 'searchlight tanks'. As the war progressed the army moved away from Lowther, and I was no longer needed. By now I was a grown up 18-years old and I had done my 'apprenticeship', and this over, I joined the commercial department at Birmingham and remained with BR until I retired in 1989.'

Top Right: *With the ruins of Penrith Castle in the background, the LMS horse team assemble outside the stable block in Ullswater Road. This station was not only on the main West Coast Line, but at the junction of what was then an important east-west cross country line linking Darlington with Workington. The LNER from Darlington came via Stainmore and Appleby, and resulted in some parcel traffic which was handled by a horse van painted in joint LMS/LNE lettering.*

Middle Right: *Seen during a lunch break at Penrith Goods Warehouse in 1942, the parcels and cartage team pose for the camera. One of the ladies (who was employed as a 'van boy') actually had the job of assisting her husband.*

Bottom Right: *Motor lorries came late to Penrith in the LMS era, although there had been a small Leyland truck based at the station in LNWR days. In 1939 a Morris Commercial platform truck was received, followed by a Fordson A type. All R. Baddeley Collection*

Top Left: *It was very much a family affair in the LMS Road Motor Department with father following son. This trio of photographs shows the Hawksworth family from Bradford, commencing with George Hawksworth and his prize winning horse. Note the pride with which the horse is displayed, and the way it is superbly decorated.*

Middle Left: *After World War I there was a move to mechanisation, and due to the proximity of Karrier Motors in Huddersfield, a large number of motor lorries were introduced into the Bradford District. Here a 3-ton Karrier with a Midland-style cab is being loaded with a large water valve destined for County Durham.*

Bottom Left: *This view dates from the 1930s, and shows the next two generations of the family standing by a Midland-cabbed Karrier (RO 914) outside the family home.* All Hawksworth Collection

John Campbell, who worked on the former Highland Section between 1941 and 1945 recounts difficulties with his Station-master who seemed to regard the station lorry as his own private vehicle. 'I had been working at Port Glasgow for several years, although I originally came from a rural district in Perthshire. After an injury during a bombing raid, I was offered the chance of light duties in the country, which I suspect was as much to help restore my nerves as it was my injuries. As it turned out the job was quite heavy and it involved using a Karrier CY 2-tonner to take hand-grenades, ammunition and jerry cans full of petrol to a nearby army training ground. This was of course in addition to the normal railway delivery work. The working day was rarely less than 10-hours and often more than 12. As it happened my first duty was 'calling up', in which I had to run round and pick up all the station staff, including the Station-master who had lodgings in a cottage some two miles from the station. He insisted that he travelled in the cab, and I often had to wait until he'd finished breakfast. He was not unknown to 'hire the lorry' to help move the belongings of army officers who were billeted in nearby villages, especially after the camp was established and the officers quarters had been built. He also asked me to do about five or six house removals, run 20 miles to the coast for a load of fish, and help on the moors to carry beaters to the grouse shoots during the season. I am not sure if he ever charged for this work, nor (if he did) whether the money went in to the cash book, but I always had plenty of work to do - and that was what they called light duties!'

David Meaden recalls his days in the service writing:- 'Although I started work on 1st January 1951, some three years after the LMS had been brought into British Railways, Willesden Goods Depot was still very much run as an LMS depot. I was just 15-years-old when I started as a Van Guard with a driver called Bill Buckland and from him I was to learn the right way to do a job. This was to take me safely through 43 years working on the railway. We had a 6-ton Mechanical Horse (GAR 717) with a petrol engine, a tongue and grooved wooden cab, and a bulbous horn. I also remember the cranked starter because it was my job to get the engine on the compression stroke. I also recall you had to be very careful where you placed your thumb on the starting handle.

During the winter months the cooling water for the engine had to be drained after each shift, this was to prevent the engines from freezing as Anti-Freeze was not available. After clocking on at 7:30am the next day, I would have the job to fill the radiator with water, using gallon cans. The radiator filler was inside the cab, the engine being directly beneath the engine casing. The engine was the only form of heating in the cab when the engine had warmed up, primitive but ideal at times. After a couple of months under unofficial tuition from Bill, I would fill and start the engine so that it was warm when he arrived.

My duties as the van boy were to help and assist the driver by looking after the goods we carried on our rounds. In time extra duties were added such as roping on loads, after Bill taught me how to tie different knots. In the 18 months I was a van boy we only ever lost one load from the dray. This was 2-tons of greased steel rope that slipped the ropes on a bumpy road. Bill also allowed me to practice coupling and un-coupling the dray and also learn the art of reversing. Driving came next, and I enjoyed the versatility of the Scammell Mechanical Horse that could go into places where a 4-wheeler had no chance.

As we did not have a permanent round, we would get a different delivery every day such as a container load. These jobs were very interesting, as were the various places we would go. When the container was loaded we would go to have it weighed at the weigh-bridge, then we went to get the delivery notes for our destination. One of my favourite places was Walters Palm Toffee in Acton, where we delivered container loads of tins from the Metal Box Co. Park Royal was full of industry in those days. There was a firm called Caxton Steel in Cumberland Road, but unloading there could take any thing from three to five hours. Other factories were Kodak, Guinness, Park Royal Vehicles, Radio Times Printers, McVities Biscuits and H.J. Heinz. Other firms we would serve were Landis & Gyr (makers of gas meters), Beclawat, Dayton Cycles, Dulcet Confectioners, Symbol Biscuits, Acton Nut & Bolt Co, Cremola (custard powder) and Ponds (makers of Vaseline). Big firms in the Willesden area included British Thomson Houston Co. and Napiers (aero engines).

Top Right: *In the days when our roads were much quieter than today, an LMS driver often had great freedom - that is until the traffic superintendent caught up with you. In this scene the driver of an AEC Y-Type (JH 2165) on the Furniture Removal Service has been tracked down and asked for a report.* R. Fysh Collection

Middle Right: *Allocated to the LMS during World War II, this Leyland 8-wheeler (DKT 658) was predominantly used for steel transportation. Fleet number 2881B carries white markings on the leading edges and wheel arches, and is fitted with ARP regulation lights.* R. Fysh Collection

Bottom Right: *This LMS Morris Commercial has been converted by Derby Works into an Airfield Rapid Defence Unit during the dark days of World War II. It was one of 30 such conversions undertaken for the RAF at short notice when invasion seemed a real threat.* LMS Official

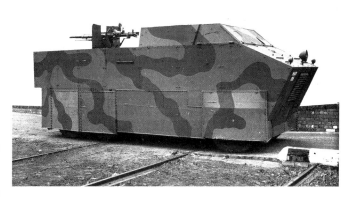

ACKNOWLEDGEMENTS

This book could not have been produced without the kind assistance of:

Robert & Elaine Baddeley
Ron Buckland
John Campbell
Jeff College
Robert Fysh
David Gladwin
G. Hawksworth
David Jenkinson
A. J. Ludlam
John McGarry
Brian Madeley
David Meaden
The Mechanical Horse Club
The National Railway Museum
Arfon Roberts
Keith Roberts
Matthew & Bryony Richardson
P. Stoneman
Stuart Shelton
Louise Tarn
David Townend

Above: *An experiment that deserved far greater development was the LMS Karrier-Ro-rail bus. This innovative concept featured a Karrier Chaser chassis and a Cravens B26C body. Registered UR 7924 and given fleet number 1RF, this bus entered service on 28th November 1930. As its name implies, it could traverse road or rail, and was really a big step forward in integrated transport. The LMS decided to test it on the Stratford & Midland Joint Line running a service to their recently acquired Welcombe Hotel in Stratford-upon-Avon. However the test was not a great success and LMS never really pursued the concept and the bus was withdrawn after it fractured an axle in July 1932. LMS Official*